THE PARABLES OF THE KINGDOM

The Parables
of the Kingdom

by

Robert Farrar Capon

WILLIAM B. EERDMANS PUBLISHING COMPANY
GRAND RAPIDS, MICHIGAN

Contents

A Word about Parables   1

PART 1   **Parables and the Paradox of Power**   **13**

CHAPTER ONE   Right-handed and Left-handed Power   15

CHAPTER TWO   The Frame of the Gospel Picture   28

CHAPTER THREE   The Temptation and the Ascension   37

PART 2   **The Parables of the Kingdom**   **51**

CHAPTER FOUR   The Ministry before the Parables   53

CHAPTER FIVE   The Sower: The Watershed of the Parables   61

CHAPTER SIX   The Sower, Continued   71

THE PARABLES OF THE KINGDOM

CHAPTER SEVEN   The Lamp and the Growing Seed   87

CHAPTER EIGHT   The Weeds   97

CHAPTER NINE   The Mustard Seed and the Leaven   111

CHAPTER TEN   The Interpretation of the Weeds   124

CHAPTER ELEVEN   The Treasure and the Pearl   134

CHAPTER TWELVE   The Net   147

                   Epilogue   164

A Word about Parables

A book about the parables of Jesus faces two obstacles at the outset.

The first and most troublesome, oddly enough, is familiarity. Most people, on reading the Gospels' assertion that "Jesus spoke in parables," assume they know exactly what is meant. "Oh, yes," they say, "and a wonderful teaching device it was, too. All those unforgettables stories we're so fond of, like the Good Samaritan and the Prodigal Son." Yet their enthusiasm is narrowly based. Jesus' use of the parabolic method can hardly be limited to the mere handful of instances they remember as entertaining, agreeable, simple, and clear. Some of his parables are not stories; many are not agreeable; most are complex; and a good percentage of them produce more confusion than understanding.

Most of this book, therefore, will be devoted to the removal of the obstacle of a too-facile familiarity. Jesus spoke in strange, bizarre, disturbing ways. He balked at almost no comparison, however irreverent or unrefined. Apparently, he found nothing odd about holding up, as a mirror to God's ways, a mixed bag of questionable characters: an unjust judge, a savage king, a tipsy slave owner, an unfair

1

employer, and even a man who gives help only to bona-fide pests. Furthermore, Jesus not only spoke in parables; he thought in parables, acted in parables, and regularly insisted that what he was proclaiming could not be set forth in any way other than in parables. He was practically an ambulatory parable in and of himself: he cursed fig trees, walked on water, planted coins in fishes' mouths, and for his final act, sailed up into a cloud. In short, this book is not a routine, pious review of the parables; rather, it is a fresh, adventurous look at the parabolic words and acts of Jesus in the larger light of their entire gospel and biblical context.

Mentioning the Bible as a whole, however, brings me to the second of the obstacles: the doubt that exists in the minds of many people as to whether anything fresh or adventurous can ever be said about Scripture by one who, as I do, views it as inspired by God. Let me try to remove that difficulty by making my own position clear.

"I do believe the Holy Scriptures of the Old and New Testaments to be the Word of God and to contain all things necessary to salvation. . . ." So read the words of the ordination oath that I took many years ago and that I am still happy to keep. I suppose it may sound, to both believer and unbeliever, like one of those bell-book-and-candle pronouncements designed to end discussion, but as far as I am concerned, it was and still is the essential precondition of my biblical study. Precisely because it forbids the neglect of even the oddest bit of Scripture, I find it nothing less than the taproot of an endlessly refreshing openness to all the wonderful, perplexing, and intriguing words by which the Word himself has spoken.

Accepting the Bible as inspired is a bit like receiving an entire collection of one's grandfather's writings. Suppose, for example, that on opening such a treasure, I found it to contain everything my grandfather ever wrote: letters, poems, recipes, essays, short stories, diaries, family histories. And suppose further that I was fully convinced not only that they were authentically his but that he had sent them for the express purpose of providing me with everything he wanted me to know both about himself and about our relationship. Far from putting an end to my study of his words, those convictions would be the very thing that started me wrestling with them in earnest.

And not just to be able to spout his words or to confirm what I already thought. Indeed, I would be well advised to approach them with as open a mind as possible, always ready to sit loose to what *I* had decided about him and simply to listen to *him*. It should be only after long study and repeated readings that I would dare to conclude what any particular passage meant, let alone what the entire thrust of his writing was. With such a wildly various collection, there would always be a temptation to let my own sense of what he was up to get in the way of what he himself really had in mind.

I might, for example, decide that, while his brief aphorisms lay close to the heart of the man, his longer stories had little to teach me about him. That would be a mistake; all that this conclusion would actually show was that I had a liking for agreeable bits of information served up on small plates but balked at the labor of trying to take his meaning when he expressed himself by putting on a feast of strange fictions. Or I might decide that only his serious metaphysical writings, and not his strictures on the proper way to make gravy, truly revealed the man. In the case of this particular grandfather, that would be an even bigger mistake: if there was ever a place where he disclosed himself as the lover of creation he really was, it was in the kitchen. Without a willingness to wade through his recipes, a reader would miss a good half of his charm.

3

So too with Scripture. Often when people try to say what the Bible is about, they let their own mindset ride roughshod over what actually lies on the pages. For examples: convinced in advance that the Bible is about God or Morals or Religion or Spirituality or Salvation or some other capital-letter Subject, they feel compelled to interpret everything in it in a commensurate way. To a degree, of course, that is a perfectly proper approach, but it has some catches to it. For one thing, it puts *their notion* of what God, or Morals, or Religion, or whatever is all about in the position of calling the tune as to what Scripture may possibly mean — or even of being the deciding factor as to whether they can listen to what it is saying at all. Jesus, for example, was rejected by his contemporaries not because he claimed to be the Messiah but because, in their view, he didn't make a suitably messianic claim. "Too bad for God," they seemed to say. "He may want a dying Christ, but we happen to know that Christs don't die."

For another thing, people's notions of the really big scriptural Subject can be quite beside the point. Suppose, by way of illustration, they were to decide that the Bible is a book about God. Harmless enough, you think? Look at how many difficulties even so apparently correct a statement can give them — and how many otherwise open scriptural doors it forces them to close. Such a position can easily lead them to expect that on every page they will find the subject of God addressed — or if it is not, that they will find there some other subject that is at least worthy of him (as they understand worthiness, of course). But that is a tricky proposition. In the Gospel of John, we read, "No man has seen God at any time; the only begotten Son [many texts read *God*], who is in the bosom of the Father, *he* has said the last word about him" (1:18). Only Jesus, apparently, is the full revelation of what God is and does; any notions we come up with are always partial, frequently misleading, and sometimes completely off the mark.

In the Bible, as a matter of fact, God does so many ungodly things — like not remembering our sins, erasing the quite correct handwriting against us, and becoming sin for us — that the only safe course is to come to Scripture with as few stipulations as possible. God used his own style manual, not ours, in the promulgation of his Word.

Openness, therefore, is the major requirement for approaching the Scriptures. And nowhere in the Bible is an un-made-up mind more called for than when reading the parables of Jesus. Indeed, if I were forced to give a short answer to the question "What is the Bible as a whole about?" I think I would ignore all the subjects mentioned so far and base my reply squarely on those parables. If they have a single subject at all, it is quite plainly the kingdom of God. Therefore, even though my answer would sound like no usual formulation at all, I would say that the Bible is about the mystery of the kingdom — a mystery that, by definition, is something well hidden and not at all likely to be grasped by plausibility-loving minds.

Jesus, when he was asked why he constantly used parables, why he so habitually resorted to roundabout, analogical devices in his teaching — why, in fact, he said almost nothing without a parable — answered that he taught the crowds that way precisely in order that "seeing they might not see and hearing they might not understand" (Mark 4:12). True enough, when he was alone with his disciples, he spoke more plainly — giving them, he claimed, nothing less than the mystery itself. But it is hard to see that such directness had a different result. On three separate occasions, for instance, he spoke quite clearly about the certainly of his dying and rising at Jerusalem, but when he came to those mighty acts themselves, his disciples might as well never have heard a word he

5

said. The mystery of the kingdom, it seems, is a *radical* mystery: even when you tell people about it in so many words, it remains permanently intractable to all their attempts to make sense of it.

In any case, a close examination of Jesus' parables may well be the best way we have of ensuring that we will be listening to what he himself has to say, instead of what we are prepared to hear — provided, that is, we are willing to take note of the almost perverse way in which he used parables.

Speaking in comparisons and teaching by means of stories are, of course, two of the oldest instructional techniques in the world. And in the hands of almost all instructors except Jesus, they are a relatively straightforward piece of business. Take an example: a professor is trying to give his students some idea of what goes on inside the atom. But because neither he nor they can actually see what he is talking about, he uses a comparison: the electrons, he tells them, are whirling around the nucleus as the planets whirl around the sun. The students suddenly see light where there was only darkness before, and the professor retires from the classroom to grateful applause.

With Jesus, however, the device of parabolic utterance is used not to explain things to people's satisfaction but to call attention to the unsatisfactoriness of all their previous explanations and understandings. Had he been the professor in the illustration, he would probably have pushed the comparison to its ultimate, mind-boggling conclusion, namely, that as the solar system is mostly great tracts of empty space, so too is matter. What they had previously thought of as solid stuff consists almost entirely of holes. He would, in other words, have done more to upset his students' understanding than to give it a helping hand.

Watch an actual instance of Jesus at his parabolic best.

In the eighteenth chapter of the Gospel of Luke, we find him addressing a group of people who are smugly content in their confidence that they are upstanding citizens — and who are convinced that anyone not exactly like themselves has no chance of making it into God's guest register. So he tells them the parable of the Pharisee and the Publican. Note not only what an insulting story it is, but also how small the prospects are that his audience will ever be able to get past its details to its point. Far from being an illustration that shines an understanding they already have on something they haven't yet figured out, it is one that is guaranteed to pop every circuit breaker in their minds.

God, Jesus informs them, is not the least bit interested in their wonderful lists of moral and religious accomplishments. Imagine the scene for a moment. You can almost hear the reaction forming in their minds: "What do you mean, God's not interested? *We* have read the Scriptures — with particular attention to the commandments. *We* happen to know he is absolutely wild about fasting, tithing, and not committing adultery." But Jesus ignores them and presses the parable for all it's worth. Not only is God going to take a dim view of all their high scores in the behaving and believing competition; he is, in fact, going to bestow the gold medal on an out-and-out crook who just waltzes into the temple, stares at his shoelaces, and does nothing more than admit as much.

But since that is not at all his audience's notion of how God should behave — since, suddenly, they now see only darkness where before they thought they had some light — since, in short, the professor has now explained something they have an utter dread of understanding, he retires from the classroom to nothing but hisses and boos.

On the way out, however, just to make sure they have not been incompletely confused, he unburdens himself of three more pieces of unwelcome instruction. First, he informs them that the kingdom of God will be given to babies sooner than to respectable religionists; second that a camel will go through a needle's eye sooner than a solid citizen will get into the kingdom; and third, that he himself, the messianic "Son of Man," is about to fulfill his messiahship by dying as a common criminal.

True enough, this last pronouncement was fairly unparabolic and was actually addressed to the disciples only. But once again, straight talk about the mystery of the kingdom produced not one bit more understanding. As Luke observed when he wrapped up the whole episode: "The disciples did not understand any of these things; the meaning of the words was hidden from them, and they did not know what Jesus was talking about" (Luke 18:34). So much for the utterances of Jesus as teaching aids.

G. K. Chesterton, who was a master of the apt illustration, once gave some sardonic advice about the limitations of parabolic discourse. He said that if you give people an analogy that they claim they do not understand, you should graciously offer them another. If they say they don't understand that either, you should oblige them with a third. But from there on, Chesterton said, if they still insist they do not understand, the only thing left is to praise them for the one truth they do have a grip on: "Yes," you tell them, "that is quite correct. You do not understand."

To put it simply, Jesus began where Chesterton left off. In resorting so often to parables, his main point was that any understanding of the kingdom his hearers could come up with would be a misunderstanding. Mention "messiah" to them, and they would picture a king on horseback, not a carpenter on a cross; mention "forgiveness" and they would start setting up rules about when it ran out. From Jesus' point of view, the sooner their misguided minds had the props knocked from under them, the better. After all their yammer about how God should or shouldn't run his own operation, getting them just to stand there with their eyes popped and their mouths shut would be a giant step forward.

We, of course, after two thousand years' exposure to Scripture in general and the Gospels in particular, might be tempted to think of ourselves as less likely to need such hard-nosed, parabolic tutelage. But Jesus still gives it to us. Despite our illusions of understanding him better than his first hearers did, we vindicate his chosen method by mis-naming — and thus misunderstanding — even the most beloved and familiar parables. The Prodigal Son, for example, is not about a boy's vices; it is about a father's forgiveness. The Laborers in the Vineyard are by no means the central characters in the story; they are hardly more than stick-figures used by Jesus to rub his hearers' noses in the outrageous grace of a vineyard owner who gives equal pay for unequal work. And if there is a Christ-figure in the parable of the Good Samaritan, it is not the Samaritan but the battered, half-dead man on the ground. Our relation-ships are defined, the parable insists, by the one who walks through our history as victim, not as medicine man. All those Good Sam Medical Centers should really have been named Man Who Fell Among Thieves Hospitals; it is the patients in their sufferings and deaths, not the help in white coats, who look more like Jesus on the cross. Jesus drives the same point home in the parable of the Great Judgment: it is precisely in the hungry, the thirsty, the estranged, the naked, the sick, and the imprisoned that we find, or ignore, the Savior himself.

With a track record of misunderstandings like those, therefore, we should probably make as few claims as possible and be content to take up the parables from scratch, begin-ning with the word itself.

The Greek for parable is *parabolé*. As far as the Gospels are concerned, the word occurs only in Matthew, Mark, and Luke. John, infrequently, uses another word, *paroimía* ("adage," or "dark saying"). Although *paroimía* has occasionally been translated "parable," neither the Greek word *parabolé* nor any parables in the usual sense appear in the Fourth Gospel.

Etymologically, a *parabolé* is simply a comparison, a putting of one thing beside another to make a point. On its face, it refers to the simple teaching device that Jesus so often transformed into something that mystified more than it informed. But standing the parabolic method on its head was not the only peculiarity in his use of it. His "parables" comprise far more than the specific utterances that the Gospel writers refer to by that name, and they occur in a surprising variety of forms.

For example, some of the parables are little more than one-liners, brief comparisons stating that the kingdom of God is like things no one ever dreamed of comparing it to: yeast, mustard seed, buried treasure secured by craftiness, fabulous jewelry purchased by mortgaging everything. On many occasions, of course, Jesus lengthened and developed the parable form into the short but marvelously complete stories to which we normally give the name. Yet for all their charm and simplicity, his story-parables are not one bit less baffling. Once again, they set forth comparisons that tend to make mincemeat of people's religious expectations. Bad people are rewarded (the Publican, the Prodigal, the Unjust Steward); good people are scolded (the Pharisee, the Elder Brother, the Diligent Workers); God's response to prayer is likened to a man getting rid of a nuisance (the Friend at Midnight); and in general, everybody's idea of who ought to be first or last is liberally doused with cold water (the Wedding Feast, the Great Judgment, Lazarus and Dives, the Narrow Door).

At other times, Jesus took his comparisons simply as he found them in the world around him. He was such an inveterate devotee of likening things to each other that these casual parables often seem to be little more than his natural habit of speaking. For example, he could mockingly contrast people's disinterest in the coming kingdom with their keen enthusiasm for weather-prediction. Or he could take some more or less current event, like the collapse of the Tower of Siloam, and use it to illustrate a point. Finally, he was not above the occasional dramatized parable in which he made his comparisons not by means of words but by acting them out — for instance, the Cursing of the Fig Tree and the Coin in the Fish's Mouth.

In any case, speaking in parables was second nature to Jesus, and it quickly became the hallmark of his teaching style. At the beginning of the Gospel of Mark in fact — after only a handful of statements actually called parables have been recorded — the author says that Jesus used many other parables, and that he would not speak to the people without using a parable (Mark 4:33-34). Clearly then, if we want to hear the actual ticking of Jesus' mind, we can hardly do better than to study his parabolic words and acts over and over — with our minds open not only to learning but to joy.

PART ONE

PARABLES AND THE PARADOX OF POWER

CHAPTER ONE

Right-handed and Left-handed Power

A few pages back, I grudgingly gave a short answer to the question of what the Bible is about. If Scripture has a single subject at all, I said, it is the mystery of the kingdom of God. Now I want to reformulate that answer in a way that will bring us not only to the parables of Jesus but also to the classification I propose to use in discussing them. If I may try your patience just a bit, let me do it by throwing you a long, slow curve.

Most authors tip their hand as to what they are really up to in their last chapters. The Holy Spirit, it seems to me, is no exception. The last book of the Bible is a gold mine of images for what God has had in mind all along. Therefore, I can think of no better way of reformulating my answer than to lean heavily on the imagery of the Revelation of St. John the Divine. Accordingly, my new version of what the Bible is about reads as follows: it is about the mystery by which the power of God works to form this world into the Holy City, the New Jerusalem that comes down out of heaven from God, prepared as a bride adorned for her husband.

Note, if you will, how much distance that puts between

us and certain customary notions of the main subject of Scripture. It means that it is not about someplace else called heaven, nor about somebody at a distance called God. Rather, it is about *this place here,* in all its *this*ness and placiness, and about the intimate and immediate Holy One who, *at no distance from us at all,* moves mysteriously to make creation true both to itself and to him. That, I take it, is the force of phrases like "the city of God" and "the kingdom of God." They say to me that the Bible is concerned with the perfecting of what God made, not with the trashing of it — with the resurrection of its native harmonies and orders, not with the replacement of them by something alien. To be sure, "city" and "kingdom" are different images, with differing lights to shed on the mystery; but because they are both such marvelously earthy revelations of what God wants this world to become, I intend to use them interchangeably throughout this book.

In any case, whether in terms of city or kingdom, the question immediately arises, "How does God get the job done? What does the Bible have to say about the way he uses his power to achieve his ends?"

On theoretical presumptions, of course, God has all the power he needs to do anything he wants any time he chooses. But such theorizing is a very unscriptural way to approach the subject. It has exactly that let's-sit-the-Bible-down-and-read-it-a-theology-lecture attitude that does nothing but produce frustration with what is actually in the book. Come to Scripture with a nice, respectable notion of an omnipotent God and see what it gets you. Problems, that's what. Problems like: If God has the ability to turn the world into the city, why is he taking his own sweet time about it? Or: If the Bible is about an almighty, all-smart God, why is it so full of divine indirection and delay? Or to say it flat out: If God wants to turn this messed-up world

16

into a city or a kingdom, why doesn't he just knock some heads together, put all the baddies under a large, flat rock, and get on with the job?

The Bible does, of course, have one recorded instance of God's having proposed just such harsh treatment: the narrative of the Flood in the Book of Genesis. But even that story — especially that story — has little comfort in it for theology buffs who like their omnipotence straight up. Notice how it goes.

God, having found all human attempts to build the city hopeless, decides simply to wash everybody but Noah down the drain. By the end of the story, however — when the final, scriptural point of the episode is made — it turns out to reveal a different notion of power entirely: God says he is never going to do anything like that again. He says that his answer to the evil that keeps the world from becoming the city of God will not, paradoxically, involve direct intervention on behalf of the city. Instead, he makes a covenant of nonintervention with the world: *he sets his bow in the cloud* — the symbolic development of which could be either that he hangs all his effective weapons against wickedness up on the wall or, more bizarrely still, that he points them skyward, at himself instead of us.

After that — to the consternation of generations of tub-thumpers for a hard-line God — the Bible becomes practically a rhapsody of indirection. God tells Abraham that he still intends to build the city but proposes an exceedingly strange way of going about it. He says he has infallible plans for the redeemed community but then proceeds to insist it be formed not at some reasonable site, but on the road — and among the future children of a man who hasn't a single descendant to his name. Furthermore, even when Abraham's childlessness is remedied and God does indeed have a people with whom to build the city, he

17

makes them spend an inordinate amount of time in slavery, wandering, and warfare before he selects a suitable piece of real estate for the venture. Finally, when he does get around to providing them with an actual location, it remains theirs (rather tenuously at that) for only a few hundred years — hardly longer, it seems, than he felt necessary to engrave Jerusalem as an image on their corporate imagination. They certainly did not possess it long enough, or with sufficient success, for anyone to claim that the city definitively had been built.

As Christians believe, though, God did eventually show up on the property himself for the express purpose of completing the project. In the person of Jesus, the messianic King, he announced that he was bringing in the kingdom and, in general, accomplishing once and for all every last eternal purpose he ever had for the world. And, as Christians also believe, he did just that. But at the end of all the doing, he simply disappeared, leaving — as far as anybody has been able to see in the two thousand or so years since — no apparent city, no effective kingdom able to make the world straighten up and fly right. The whole operation began as a mystery, continued as a mystery, came to fruition as a mystery, and to this day continues to function as a mystery. Since Noah, God has evidently had almost no interest in using direct power to fix up the world.

Why? you ask. Well, the first answer is, I don't know, and neither does anyone else. God's reasons are even more hidden than his methods. But I have seen enough of the results of direct intervention to make me rather glad that he seems, for whatever reason, to have lost interest in it.

Direct, straight-line, intervening power does, of course, many uses. With it, you can lift the spaghetti from the your mouth, wipe the sauce off your slacks, carry the dry cleaners, and perhaps even make enough

18

money to ransom them back. Indeed, straight-line power ("use the force you need to get the result you want") is responsible for almost everything that happens in the world. And the beauty of it is, it works. From removing the dust with a cloth to removing your enemy with a .45, it achieves its ends in sensible, effective, easily understood ways.

Unfortunately, it has a whopping limitation. If you take the view that one of the chief objects in life is to remain in loving relationships with other people, straight-line power becomes useless. Oh, admittedly, you can snatch your baby boy away from the edge of a cliff and not have a broken relationship on your hands. But just try interfering with his plans for the season when he is twenty, and see what happens, especially if his chosen plans play havoc with your own. Suppose he makes unauthorized use of your car, and you use a little straight-line verbal power to scare him out of doing it again. Well and good. But suppose further that he does it again anyway — and again and again and again. What do you do next if you are committed to straight-line power? You raise your voice a little more nastily each time till you can't shout any louder. And then you beat him (if you are stronger than he is) until you can't beat any harder. Then you chain him to a radiator till. . . . But you see the point. At some very early crux in that difficult, personal relationship, the whole thing will be destroyed unless you — who, on any reasonable view, should be allowed to use straight-line power — simply refuse to use it; unless, in other words, you decide that instead of dishing out justifiable pain and punishment, you are willing, quite foolishly, to take a beating yourself.

But such a paradoxical exercise of power, please note, is a hundred and eighty degrees away from the straight-line variety. It is, to introduce a phrase from Luther, left-handed power. Unlike the power of the right hand (which, interestingly enough, is governed by the logical, plausibility-loving left hemisphere of the brain), left-handed power is guided by the more intuitive, open, and imaginative right side of the brain. Left-handed power, in other words, is precisely paradoxical power: power that looks for all the world like weakness, intervention that seems indistinguishable from nonintervention. More than that, it is guaranteed to stop no determined evildoers whatsoever. It might, of course, touch and soften their hearts. But then again, it might not. It certainly didn't for Jesus; and if you decide to use it, you should be quite clear that it probably won't for you either. The only thing it does insure is that you will not — even after your chin has been bashed in — have made the mistake of closing any interpersonal doors from your side.

Which may not, at first glance, seem like much of a thing to insure, let alone like an exercise worthy of the name of power. But when you come to think of it, it *is* power — so much power, in fact, that it is the only thing in the world that evil can't touch. God in Christ died forgiving. With the dead body of Jesus, he wedged open the door between himself and the world and said, "There! Just try and get me to take *that* back!"

And here is where this long, slow curve starts to curl in over the plate. Just as, in the whole of the Bible, it takes a while before God's preference for paradoxical rather than straight-line power manifests itself — just as God seems to do a lot of right-handed pushing and shoving before he does the left-handed but ultimately saving thing on the cross — so too it seems that, for quite some time, Jesus puts himself forth in the Gospels as a plausible, intervening, advice-giving, miracle-working Messiah before he finally reveals himself as a dying, rising, and disappearing one. Indeed, it is one of the premises of this book that if the parables are examined in the context of the development of Jesus' thinking on the subjects of power and its use, light will be shed both on them and on him.

Accordingly, I divide the parables into three groups. The first group — the short, almost one-sentence *parables of the kingdom* that occur in the Gospels prior to the Feeding of the Five Thousand — is the subject of this book. In subsequent volumes, I shall deal with the longer, story-length *parables of grace* (as I shall call them) that occur between the Feeding and the Triumphal Entry into Jerusalem, and with the stern, strange *parables of judgment* that the Gospel writers set mostly between the Entry and the Crucifixion.

One question about this classification arises immediately: Why make the Feeding of the Five Thousand a pivotal point? Well, first of all, because it is the only miracle of Jesus that is reported in all four Gospels; better and closer-to-the-event minds than yours or mine have already singled it out for unique attention. But second, if it is examined closely, it turns out to be pivotal not only in people's attitudes toward Jesus but also in his own thinking about himself.

No one can prove anything about Jesus' innermost, unexpressed thoughts, of course, but just for a moment consider this. In the early part of his ministry Jesus put himself forth pretty much as the kind of messiah people could take a liking to: a wonder-working rabbi who, by a combination of miracles and good teaching, sounded like the answer to everybody's prayers. But even at the start he did not buy into that formula completely. His miracles were often followed by stern warnings not to make them (or him) known — hardly the sort of thing to delight the heart of a sensible press agent — and his teaching was largely given in parables nobody understood. From the very beginning, in other words, Jesus seems to have had second thoughts about the style in which he was exercising power, and especially about how that style might easily give people the impression he was engaged in little more than a patch job on the world.

But there is more. Unlike many miracle workers who actually make a point of offering to work miracles — or who at least give the impression that miracles are what it's all about and stake their claim to attention precisely on that basis — Jesus is curiously reluctant about doing his "signs." (An important note here: the Greek word usually translated "miracle" does not have miraculous overtones; it is simply the ordinary word for "sign," *sēmeíon*.) Not only does Jesus play down his signs; it almost seems that he doesn't do them unless they are practically wrung out of him by others. He looks for all the world like a kind of walking cafeteria table of power from which people serve themselves with hardly a by-your-leave. (The woman with the issue of blood who, unbeknownst to Jesus, touched the hem of his garment is perhaps the clearest case; but the "involuntariness," or at least the offhandedness of his miracles, is manifest time and again.)

And — to come to the point at last — I think it is in the Feeding of the Five Thousand that his reluctance about giving signs becomes decisively manifest. Consider: At the end of a long day in the middle of nowhere, Jesus' disciples come and nag him about the obvious facts that it is late and that he has a hungry crowd on his hands. Their suggestion is to send the people packing before it gets dark; but Jesus, seemingly exhausted by the day, tells them to handle matters themselves and go buy some food. They complain they don't have enough money. They even give him a caterer's estimate of the cost. Finally, as if he is more interested in solving their problem than the crowd's, he reluctantly involves himself in the project. "How much food have you actually got?" he asks them. They say, "Five loaves and two fishes."

The rest, of course, is history. But can anyone seriously

conclude from such an account that the Feeding was part of his master plan for the day? Doesn't it read as if he simply dragged his feet as long as he could before doing anything — as if it was only when nothing else worked that he finally uncovered himself as the messianic cafeteria counter and let them take as much as they wanted? Indeed, it seems that even while the miracle was in progress he made as little of it as possible: no hocus-pocus, no long prayers, no holy exhortations — just break it up and pass it out. The whole thing was so underplayed that the bread probably reached the back row of the crowd before the first row figured out what was happening.

But — and here is where the Feeding manifests its pivotal nature — all the rows eventually did figure it out. And when they did, Jesus' reaction was to become something very like unglued. Matthew and Mark depict him hurriedly ordering his disciples to get into the boat and go on ahead of him to Bethsaida. In John, the disciples seem to embark of their own accord, but the people in the crowd stay around with a vengeance. They get the brilliant idea that anybody who can produce food like that ought to be made king — by force, if necessary.

In any case, the next thing Jesus does is to send the crowd away and head for the hills himself. He prays. For a long time. Meanwhile, a storm comes up on the lake (Jesus could see the disciples having trouble rowing, so this had to be sometime before dark). So what does he do? He keeps on praying. In fact, he prays till between three and six in the morning; at which point, according to Mark, he walks out on the water to his disciples and acts as if he is going to pass them by. Needless to say, they do a little thinking about ghosts and then proceed straight to rather a lot of screaming. Jesus simply tells them to cheer up: "It's me," he says, "don't be afraid." Once again, the rest is history:

not only the calming of the storm, but the disciples' sudden realization that they were more afraid of him than of any wind that ever blew.

But I think something else is also history: the galvanizing effect the whole day and night had on Jesus' thoughts about messiahship and power. It seems to me that from the Feeding of the Five Thousand on, he had a much firmer grip on the truth that the Messiah was not going to save the world by miraculous, Band-Aid interventions: a storm calmed here, a crowd fed there, a mother-in-law cured back down the road. Rather, it was going to be saved by means of a deeper, darker, left-handed mystery, at the center of which lay his own death.

In any case, it is only after the Feeding that his talk about dying actually begins. In Luke it starts a mere three verses later, at 9:21. In Matthew, the Feeding is in chapter 14 and the first prophecy of his death in chapter 16. In Mark, the chapters are 6 and 8 respectively. In all three, moreover, the death-talk is immediately followed by the Transfiguration — and that, of course, by the downhill slide of his once-upbeat career into the mystery of Good Friday and Easter.

Which brings us to a second question — perhaps difficulty is a better word — that Christians sometimes have when it is suggested that Jesus' thinking about his life and work actually underwent development during the course of his ministry. Because they believe he is in fact God incarnate, they have problems with such an apparent limitation of the divine omniscience. Their belief leads them, unless they formulate their theology about it very carefully indeed, to think that development is somehow an unsuitable process for the Redeemer to undergo.

What they need to do, of course, is to make some distinctions. Jesus, as the Word made flesh, is both God and man and he possesses both of those natures "without confusion, without change, without division, and without separation" (to use the words of the Chalcedonian definition). That means, among other things, that while it is perfectly proper to use the attributes of either nature when you are talking about the Person who is both (for instance: *the carpenter of Nazareth made the world; God died on the cross*), you must be careful not to scramble the two natures when you are speaking of how each one operates in its own proper sphere (thus: *God, as God, does not die; Jesus, in his human mind, is not omniscient*).

The fact that Jesus is God in man means exactly that: he is true God, genuine Deity, in an equally genuine and therefore complete, even *mere* humanity. In his divine mind, for example, God the Son — the Second Person of the Trinity, the Incarnate Lord — knows absolutely everything; but in his human mind — in the only mind, we believe, through which that same Lord finally, authoritatively, and personally reveals himself in this world — Jesus cannot help but be absolutely ignorant of, say, first-century Chinese, modern French, Jeffersonian democracy, and nuclear physics. The inevitable condition of a historical incarnation — that he must have a particular human body and mind in an equally particular place and time — precludes his being either Superman or Mr. Know-It-All.

The upshot of this is that some Christians, failing to make such distinctions rigorously enough, fall into the trap of thinking that if Jesus is really God, it is somehow unfitting or even irreverent to posit any development at all, even in his human mind. They feel obliged to maintain that, right from the beginning, he had everything figured out completely and that any apparent developments in his awareness were simply due to the way he deferred to our slow-wittedness by doling out his revelations piece by piece. But to put it that way is to expose their fallacy. "From what beginning?"

such theologians should be asked. Presumably, they are thinking of the beginning of his public ministry or perhaps of those first words of his at age twelve when he told his parents he had to be "about his Father's business." But those are plainly not beginnings enough.

Back at the real beginning of his earthly ministry — at the annunciation, say, or in the stable at Bethlehem — how much did he know about anything? Not only was he ignorant, in the only human mind he had, of Chinese and French; he didn't even know Aramaic. *That* knowledge, since he was truly human, would come only in the way it came to all the other truly human little boys born at the same time: by the natural processes of human development.

More to the point, as a baby he was equally ignorant not only of the implausible, left-handed style of exercising power, but even of the simpler, more logical, right-handed one. Truly orthodox, classical Christian theology does not require us to posit for Jesus a human mind that works by freakish stunts. We may posit all the influences of the Holy Spirit upon him that we care to, but it is simply against the rules to turn that mind into a third something-or-other that is neither divine nor human. Jesus has two unconfused, unchanged, undivided, unseparated natures in one Person. He is not a metaphysical scrambled egg.

This chapter, however, is running the danger of becoming nothing but a series of long, slow curves, so let me end it with one pitch right to the strike zone. The last four paragraphs have been about theology — an enterprise that, despite the oftentimes homicidal urgency Christians attach to it, has yet to save anybody. What saves us is Jesus, and the way we lay hold of that salvation is by *faith*. And faith is something that, throughout this book, I shall resolutely refuse to let mean anything other than *trusting Jesus*. It is simply saying yes to him rather than no. It is, at its root, a mere "uh-huh" to him personally. It does not necessarily involve any particular theological structure or formulation; it does not entail any particular degree of emotional fervor; and above all, it does not depend on any specific repertoire of good works — physical, mental, or moral. It's just, "Yes, Jesus" till we die — just letting the power of his resurrection do, in our deaths, what it has already done in his.

My purpose in saying this so strongly, however, is not simply to alert you to some little band of intellectuals called theologians who may try to talk you into thinking otherwise. Such types exist, of course, but they are usually such bores that all they do is talk you out of wanting even to breathe. No, the reason for my vehemence is that *all* of us are theologians. Every one of us would rather choose the right-handed logicalities of theology over the left-handed mystery of faith. Any day of the week — and twice on Sundays, often enough — we will labor with might and main to take the only thing that can save anyone and reduce it to a set of theological club rules designed to exclude almost everyone.

Christian theology, however, never is and never can be anything more than the thoughts that Christians have (alone or with others) *after* they have said yes to Jesus. Sure, it can be a thrilling subject. Of course, it is something you can do well or badly — or even get right or wrong. And naturally, it is one of the great fun things to do on weekends when your kidney stones aren't acting up. Actually, it is almost exactly like another important human subject that meets all the same criteria: wind-surfing. Everybody admires it, and plenty of people try it. But the number of people who can do it well is even smaller than the number who can do it without making fools of themselves.

Trust Jesus, then. After that, theologize all you want. Just don't lose your sense of humor if your theological surfboard deposits you unceremoniously in the drink.

CHAPTER TWO

The Frame of the Gospel Picture

Before moving on to the parables of the kingdom, I think it is important to spend a little more time driving home the idea that the ministry of Jesus, taken in its entirety, is the manifestation of God's deep preference for a left-handed, mysterious exercise of power as opposed to a right-handed, plausible one. And I think that's so because while it is obvious from the Gospels that Jesus' real program — his ultimate saving action on behalf of the world — is his death and resurrection, too many Christians seem excessively fond of preaching a different message. They talk as if his miraculous cures and assorted other right-handed interventions were the heart of his program. What they do not say, but what the New Testament clearly maintains, is that his displays of straight-line power were not his program at all, but only the *signs* of it.

Consider therefore the two "parabolic events" — as I shall call them here — with which the Gospel writers actually frame the whole of Jesus' active ministry: the Temptation in the Wilderness and the Ascent into Heaven. Both deal specifically with the messianic use of power. In the former, the devil pleads (rather convincingly, too) for Jesus to do three altogether sensible things: to use his might to turn stones into bread (and by extension, to do something useful about human hunger); to display his power over death in a well-staged spectacle that would get people's attention; and last and most important, to use the devil's own eminently practical, right-handed methods for getting the world to shape up. Moreover, at the Ascension, the disciples — who even as late as forty days after the resurrection still seem not to have grasped what Jesus spent three years telling them — ask him if he will now at last put aside the mystery and openly restore the kingdom to Israel. To which Jesus gives two answers. The first is a rebuke: such matters, he tells them, are not theirs to know. The second is an action: to underscore the fact that what he is doing will not be done in any such recognizable fashion, he simply ascends and disappears.

Two sets of questions arise out of the last paragraph. You may well wonder whether I haven't perhaps overstated myself about the "framing" function of these two episodes, and you may have your doubts as to the propriety of my calling them "parabolic events." Let me deal with each problem in order.

I am aware that the Temptation story appears only in Matthew, Mark (briefly), and Luke. Its absence from John, however, does not detract from my thesis. John omits a number of important events in Jesus' life, but he deals with their import or ramifications in other ways and contexts. He does not, for example, include a narration of the institution of the Eucharist; yet he devotes more space (chapters 13 through 17) to the Last Supper than the other three writers put together.

Not only that, but in chapter 6, after the Feeding of the Five Thousand, John includes the very cornerstone of eucharistic doctrine: Jesus' proclamation of himself as the

Bread of Life. Accordingly, my own disposition when I find something "missing" from John is to look for the place (or places) where he works it in under another guise. The Transfiguration, for instance, seems to be adumbrated by John in Jesus' great high-priestly prayer in chapter 17. No other place in the Gospels better manifests in discourse what the Transfiguration account in the synoptics portrays in narrative, namely, that Jesus' divine unity with the Father is the very foundation of his relationship with both the disciples and the world.

In the case of the Temptation narrative, therefore, we need to ask where its equivalent occurs in John. Is there any place where the same debate over power occurs — where tempting voices urge Jesus to use plausible, right-handed power and where he responds by dragging his feet with mysterious left-handed responses?

When you put the question that way, the answer becomes obvious: the Johannine Temptation is contained, like the Johannine eucharistic passages, in chapter 6 of the Gospel. Consider: The crowd that witnessed the Feeding of the Five Thousand catches up with Jesus the next day in Capernaum and starts feeding him all sorts of straight-lines in the hope that he will respond with a public commitment to using his now-obvious power in an intelligible, right-handed way. Their whole performance is worthy of the devil himself: with condescending pieties fronting for their firm belief that they, and not Jesus, know best how to run a tight messianic ship, they press him harder and harder to make some plausible demonstration.

"Our ancestors ate manna in the desert," they remind him. "What will you do to match that?" Jesus, though, retreats deeper and deeper into mystery: "What Moses gave you," he tells them, "was not the bread from heaven; *I* am the bread of life." And he continues in that vein until he loses not only his audience but many of his disciples as well.

At the end only the twelve are left — and with only dumb, blind faith keeping them there at that. When Jesus asks them if they, too, want to go away, Peter answers, "Lord, to whom can we go? You have the words of eternal life." But Peter, unable as usual to keep quiet, goes on to blow his commitment with some gratuitous babble: " . . . and we have believed and known that you are the Holy One of God." Had he stopped at "believe," it might have been all right, but the claim to *know* simply gave Jesus the willies. It made him jump straight to thinking that even among his chosen twelve there was a devil — a worshiper of intelligible, right-handed power who would sooner or later betray him. John, therefore, no less than Matthew, Mark, and Luke, does full justice to the devilish trial of the Messiah.

But if that much can be said for a four-Gospel, full-court press as regards the Temptation, what about the Ascension? In particular, what about the fact that only Luke seems to record it?

Once again it strikes me that the omission of the Ascension from Matthew and Mark and especially from John is more apparent than real. As a matter of fact, I make my same argument: in one form or another, all four Gospels have the equivalent of the Ascension. For example, although the literal business of Jesus' going up in the air is not mentioned in Matthew 28:16-20, the passage describes an otherwise identical hilltop departure scene. And as I have said, it seems to me that it is precisely *departure* that lies at the root of Jesus' parabolic last act.

In Mark, on the other hand, although the Ascension does not appear in some of the oldest and best manuscript sources of the Gospels (some of these manuscripts have Mark end at chapter 16, verse 8, even before the resurrection appearances have occurred), it does appear at 16:19 in many other sources. At the very least, whatever the explanation may have been for its omission from certain fourth-century manuscripts, there was a strong feeling on the part of the early church — the group that, please note, had included "ascended into heaven" in its baptismal creed much earlier — that the Ascension scene simply had to be included in Mark.

Since the Lucan record of Jesus' being "taken up into heaven" is perfectly clear (Luke 24:51 and Acts 1:9), that leaves only the Gospel of John to reckon with. As before, I invoke my principle of looking for important missing material in the Fourth Gospel by trying to discover where John dealt with the subject thematically rather than narratively. And when I do that, far from finding John to have the least space of all devoted to the Ascension, I find him, hands-down once again, to have the most. All through the discourse at the Last Supper (John 13–17), Jesus returns over and over to the theme of his departure. True, the genius of John for dealing with several things at once is such that a good deal of what Jesus says applies as much to his crucifixion and death as it does to his ascension. But an equally great deal of it is pure departure talk: "Yet a little while and the world will see me no more" (14:19); "I am leaving, but I will come back to you" (14:28); "It is better for you that I go away" (16:7); "Father, now I am coming to you" (17:13).

Accordingly, I find the Ascension just as essential a piece of Gospel framework as the Temptation: both, it seems to me, are acted parables of power aimed at driving home — one at the end of Jesus' ministry and one at the beginning — a clear lesson about how his power is *not* going to be used. Taken seriously, they can go a long way toward keeping our otherwise easily derailed theological locomotives securely on the Gospel track.

That leaves only the question of whether calling them "parabolic events" is suitable to their importance. True enough, such a phrase, in the hands of certain biblical critics, could be a bit off-putting; some of them use the word "parabolic" to excuse themselves from the unpleasant prospect of having to deal with miraculous episodes as actual events. That, however, is not my intention. Let me make my own position clear by examining first the Ascension, then the Temptation.

The critics I refer to usually say something like this: In Jesus' time, people thought heaven was literally *up;* we, however, having abandoned the flat-earth theory, know that it is not a "place" at all — at least not one you can reach by traveling from here to there. Thus, they argue, the story of the Ascension was probably made up by Luke, or somebody, to provide a suitably parabolic interpretation of the obvious fact that Jesus wasn't around any more after the great forty days.

I have a number of objections to that kind of fast-and-loose shuffle. The first is: If the critics are willing to give Luke credit for being bright enough to *think up* the parable of the Ascension, why are they unwilling to give Jesus credit for having the cleverness and the ability to *act it out?* The answer, of course, is that they have a prejudice against miracles and will do almost anything to avoid having to posit one as a legitimate, historical event. They are entitled to that prejudice; but they are not, for my money, entitled to put it forth as a piece of biblical criticism. The Ascension just sits there on the pages of Luke, obstinately refusing to get out of the text. They don't have to like it, but they should do everyone the favor of acknowledging that their dislike is based on an a priori philosophical judgment and not on Scripture itself.

My second objection proceeds from that. The veneer of scientific respectability they put on their argument ("Heaven can't possibly be just *up*") is another dodge. Of course heaven isn't up. But if you are going to act out a cosmically significant departure, you have — even in the twentieth century — a choice of only three directions: up, down, or sideways. Of those only *up* has the parabolic significance you are after. *Down* implies the exact opposite of what you want to symbolize, and *sideways* might make people think only that you had moved to Grand Rapids.

Finally, it seems silly for these debaters to mention the flat-earth–round-earth controversy. Their whole argument attacks only a straw man. Whatever your view of terrestrial and celestial mechanics, neither Scripture nor sound theology requires you to get Jesus any further spatially than the first cloud. After that, the Ascension as an event in this world is over, and the cosmic significance of it becomes — as it was meant to be all along — the main thing.

So I am perfectly happy to take the Ascension as an event, and I am equally comfortable trying to plumb its parabolic significances to my heart's content. The two activities do not conflict in any way. Indeed, they absolutely require each other. If you insist on the Ascension as a mere happening, you miss its meaning; if you harp only on its meaning, you cut it off from history — which is the only arena in which God has revealed to us, parabolically or otherwise, his purpose.

The Temptation, on the other hand, presents fewer problems. Once again, it just sits there on the pages, refusing to apologize for its presence. To be sure, critics who have a priori objections to the devil will try, as always, to claim that the episode was the product of a fertile imagination rather than an actual happening. But that is an instance of letting your prejudices carry you into a totally pointless enterprise.

First of all, unless you are absolutely bent on doubting the obvious, the most likely candidate to have had that fertile imagination and to have disclosed the Temptation story was Jesus himself. (The devil is a possibility too, of course, but since neither the critics nor myself want to be caught dead advocating that one, let it pass.) Presumably, therefore, it was Jesus who was the original source of the Temptation narrative.

Second, unless you are unwilling to give Jesus' parabolic abilities as much credit here as elsewhere, it is altogether reasonable to expect that in recounting the whole experience of being tempted by the devil, he would cast it in suitable narrative form. It might even be, of course, that the three temptations enumerated were in fact the very ones that occurred. Indeed, it may well have been that every detail in the episode literally took place in some specific "there" and "then." But none of those problems is either capable of solution or important to solve. The significance of the whole narration is Jesus' disclosure of the great debate over messianic power, *as he experienced it.* Whether it took place at 3:00 P.M. or in Jerusalem or on a mountaintop or simply in his mind is quite secondary to the fact that it occurred in his person at the instigation of somebody or something that had a deep interest in turning the mystery of saving, left-handed power into just another right-handed, strong-arm job that would leave the world still on the skids.

Finally, there is the question of *when* Jesus informed the disciples about the Temptation. No one can prove anything. The Gospel writers simply thread in the account of it right at the beginning of his ministry, and there is no reason to doubt that that is when it happened. But it seems to me quite likely that that is not when he told them about it. They had enough trouble grasping relatively simple parabolic material like the Sower, the Yeast, and the rest. Even when he informed them later, in so many words, about his impending and utterly left-handed plan to die and rise, they still failed to comprehend. So my own choice for the point at which Jesus filled them in about the Temptation is the great forty days between the Resurrection and the Ascension. It was precisely then, when his renunciation of right-handed power was almost as clearly revealed as it ever would be, that they would have the best chance of finally seeing what he was talking about.

In any case, both the Temptation and the Ascension seem to bear up fairly well as parabolic events that frame an equally parable-filled history. Both are about the subject of power, and if I am even warm in my hunch about when Jesus revealed them, each may well have a good bit of the other mixed up in it. Time now to examine them in detail.

CHAPTER THREE

The Temptation and the Ascension

The first thing to note about the Temptation of Jesus is that it happened under the guidance of the Spirit. Mark, who mentions it by little more than title (Mark 1:12-13), nevertheless manages to include a vivid reference: the Spirit, he says, *drives out* (RSV) — or even *throws out: ekbállei* — Jesus into the desert. Matthew and Luke, who spell out the specific temptations, say that Jesus was *led (anéchthē, égeto)* by the Spirit (Matt. 4:1; Luke 4:1). All of them agree, though, that Jesus did not just wander into his confrontation with the devil. The meeting is clearly portrayed as part of a larger plan — a plan, please note, that Jesus' *human mind* may very well not have been privy to before the event.

Which raises once again a theological consideration that needs constant emphasis. Jesus, we believe, is indeed truly divine and truly human. But those two natures, while inseparably joined in God the Son, the Second Person of the Trinity, are distinct and unconfused. The Incarnate Lord is not a mishmash of divinity and humanity. There is not a scrap of human nature in his Godhead, and most important here, there is not a smitch of deity in his manhood, any more than there is in yours or mine. He came to save *us,* in *our* nature, not to put on some flashy, theandric, super-human performance that would be fundamentally irrelevant to our condition.

Accordingly, when the deity of Jesus acts or impinges upon his humanity, it does so not in the order of nature — not by souping up his humanity into something more than human — but in the order of *grace:* that is, by divine influences that empower human nature but do not tamper with it. In Scripture it is precisely the Holy Spirit, the Third Person of the Trinity, who is given credit for enabling and guiding the humanity of Jesus. For example, Jesus casts out demons not by means of some more-than-human power that he has in and of himself, but by the Spirit — by, as he puts it, the Finger of God.

Therefore, when we talk about the development of Jesus' messianic consciousness, we should stay light-years away from any suggestion that he had a kind of trap door between his divine and human minds. We should avoid, in other words, the humanity-destroying trick of positing leaks from his deity into his humanity. The influence of the Spirit alone — acting upon his human nature in no fundamentally different way than it does on ours — is quite sufficient: it covers all the biblical bases; it provides for all the divine "informing" we ever need to speak of; and it does so without turning Jesus into Superman.

Indeed, the Superman analogy is a perfect illustration of what Jesus is not. He is not from another planet but from this one. He does not have, in his human nature, powers beyond those of mortal men; instead, he is just as mortal as we are. Neither is he immune to any of our other debilities and limitations: not hunger, not thirst, not exhaustion, not exasperation, certainly not speeding locomotives, and probably not even the common cold. Above all, he is born among us as Clark Kent; he lives among us as Clark Kent; he dies as Clark Kent; and he comes forth from the tomb as Clark Kent — not as some alien hotshot in blue tights who, at the crucial moment, junks his Clark Kentness in favor of a snappier, nonhuman style of being.

Furthermore, the Superman myth provides us with an equally perfect bridge to, and handle on, the subject of the Temptation. For what is the dialogue in the wilderness if not the devil's attempt to sell Jesus a set of messianic blue tights? "If you really are the Son of God," Satan wheedles, "put a little moxie in your act. Don't just stand there (or even, unthinkably, *hang* there); *do* something. The world is going to hell in a handbasket. People are starving for food; they're wandering in mental darkness because God never gives them any straight-line demonstrations of power to latch onto; and they're suffering from the chaos of a world that could turn into a gorgeous place if only someone with enough power would smack it into line. Get into the phone booth, then, and come out swinging. With my brains and your brawn, we could really get this show on the road."

To all of this Jesus simply replies from chapters 6 and 8 of Deuteronomy, the sections recapitulating the ten commandments in chapter 5. Do you see what that means? It means that when the devil talks messiah, Jesus answers with passages that are not messianic at all, but simply addressed to humanity as such. He says, in effect, "*You* can't conceive of a messiah unless he's dedicated to a lot of superhuman, right-handed punching and interfering; but as far as I'm concerned, just plain human obedience to God's prescriptions for plain old humanity will do the messianic trick. Thank you very much, but peddle your phone booth somewhere else."

The dialogue between Jesus and the devil, you see, is a

conversation between two people who simply cannot understand what each other is saying. Satan talks right-handed power; Jesus talks left. They might as well be in different universes. As a matter of fact, they *are* in different universes: Jesus, in the only one there really is; and the devil, in the distorted, secondhand version of it that he, as the father of lies, has managed to fake out.

Still, to our discredit (we abandon our devotion to the methods of the Prince of this world very slowly indeed), the devil does strike us as having all the best lines. What he says makes sense to our inveterately right-handed souls. But what Jesus says in reply — not to mention what he ends up doing over the full course of his ministry — seems not only nonsense, but heartless nonsense at that.

Take the temptations in the order they occur in Matthew (Luke transposes the second and the third, but that makes little difference here). For the first, the devil suggests to Jesus — who after forty days of fasting has got to be hungry — that he use his messianic, Son of God power to make himself a stone sandwich right on the spot. "Do something, for earth's sake," he seems to be saying. "You have the power to wipe out not only your own hunger but the whole world's. What's wrong with using it?"

"Man shall not live by bread alone," Jesus answers, quoting Deuteronomy 8:3, "but by every word that comes out of the mouth of God."

"Now hold on a minute," Satan says (if we may give him, like members of Congress, the privilege of extending his remarks). "Not so fast. Who said anything against God? You mean you can't eat bread *and* live by God's words at the same time? If that's true, it looks like pretty bad divine planning. Look, you're going to eat something soon, aren't you?"

Jesus nods.

"Maybe you'll even have an early supper today, right? You certainly deserve it."

Jesus nods again.

"You might even stop at a delicatessen on the way home and pick up a little something, no?"

Jesus shrugs.

"Well, then. If you're going to eat soon — and if there's no necessary conflict between, say, a chopped liver on rye and obeying God — why not eat now?"

Jesus shakes his head no.

The devil thinks for a moment and then tries a different tack. "Tell me," he says, "would you turn these stones into bread, not for yourself but for some really hungry people?"

Jesus turns his hands over and back in a little gesture that says, possibly.

"Aha!" the devil says. "Then I've got you. In Leviticus 19:18, it says, 'love your neighbor as yourself.' If it's not all right to feed yourself, how can you feed others?"

Jesus yawns. The devil shifts gears.

He takes Jesus up on a pinnacle of the temple in Jerusalem. "Look," he says, "forget the bread business. I'm talking now about people's really deep spiritual needs. As I see it, the trouble with God's operation is that it's entirely too vague. I mean, if he wants people to obey him, not to mention to love him, how come he's so reluctant to give them a clear shot at seeing him in action? Everything he does is so . . . covert. And people suffer because of that. They can't help it if he made them dependent on what they see with their own eyes or experience in their own bodies. It's the old story of the donkey and the two-by-four. They're not really bad; all you have to do is give them a good whack to get their attention. How about a nice, miraculous two-by-four then? Jump down from here. Psalm 91:11-12 even guarantees God will approve: angels will catch you before

41

you hit the sidewalk, and you'll have done the world the favor of concentrating its mind a whole lot."

Jesus says, "You shall not tempt the Lord your God."

"For crying out loud," the devil complains, "this is your idea of tempting? I can't believe what I'm listening to. I hand you a first-rate messianic prophecy, and you refuse to fulfill it. Did it ever occur to you that maybe you're not the Messiah? What are you going to do, spend your entire career studiously avoiding anything that people could recognize as divine action?"

Jesus purses his lips.

"Listen," Satan says, "I can see this is getting us nowhere. Let me give you a real mountaintop experience. I want you to picture yourself on a high, high hill — so high that from the peak you can see all the kingdoms of the world. And I would also like it if we could both please drop the polite pussyfooting and just speak plainly. I admit it. I was putting you on with all that 'if you're the Son of God' stuff. I have absolutely no question about who you are. But on the other hand, neither do you have any question about who I am — and especially about the rights and privileges you gave me over this shooting match you call a world. Not that it was exactly a terrific gift: you recognized my talents by making me Prince here, but you were a bit stingy when it came to giving me the power I needed to run it.

"What I'm suggesting is that, since we both have a major investment in this operation, we stop all the bickering and, for the world's sake, make common cause. You have the power and I have the smarts. All you have to do is help me get my plans operative, and between the two of us we'll have this place turned back into Eden in six months. What do you say? Not only would it work, but it would get you one hell of a lot better press than you've had for centuries."

Jesus smiles at him, shaking his head up and down as

if to say, "That's exactly what I'm afraid of." Then he turns grim. "Look," he says, "just get out of here, huh? I take my orders from one source only, and you, Charley, are definitely not it."

But enough of the Temptation itself. Paradoxically, Jesus eventually does all the things the devil suggests. But he does them in his own time and in his own way. He turns five loaves and two fish into an all-time eatout for five thousand. This, while it is essentially the same trick as making himself a miraculous snack, is not only more of a sign but also one that serves to intensify rather than vitiate his commitment to left-handed power.

Furthermore, instead of merely circumventing death by having angels catch him (a sign, please note, that would promise nothing to the rest of us who are not messiahs), he dies as dead as anyone and then rises to become the first fruits of them that slept (a phrase that means — since no child of Adam and Eve is exempt from that sleep — abso- lutely everybody). Finally, he does indeed take up the ruler- ship of this world, but instead of doing so by the devil's device of moving in and applying strong-arm methods, he ascends and sits as King of Kings and Lord of Lords at his Father's right hand. He continues to govern, in other words, as the Wisdom of God he always was, reaching from one end of the universe to the other, and mightily and sweetly — *fortiter suaviterque* — ordering all things.

A question. Does the phrase "his Father's right hand" undo my whole case for Jesus' abiding commitment to left-handed power? Does it suggest that when all is said and done, the divine Wisdom is going to get the sweetness out of his act and revert to rockem-sockem tactics? Not to my mind, it doesn't. First of all, God as God does not have a literal right hand; the phrase is clearly a metaphor for the highest and holiest station of all. But second, the Greek simply doesn't mention "hand." It says (cf. Mark 16:19) that he enthroned himself *ek dexión tou theoú* — literally, "out of the right-sidednesses [the idiom is oddly plural] of God." Therefore, if I choose to argue that, in ascending, he declares his eternal intention to act out of the *right hemisphere of God's brain* — and thus forever to commit himself to left-handed power — who is to say me nay? "Brain" is as legitimate (and as illegitimate) an image as "hand" to apply to God; the real point is that we should feel free to *play* with the images of Scripture, letting their light fall on as many facets of experience as possible. Still, if that sort of argument strikes you as over the foul line, let it pass. Go directly to the Ascension.

The first thing to be said about Jesus' last earthly act is that it was utterly consistent with the rest of his ministry. It was, from the point of view of exercising power, a bizarre and paradoxical conclusion to a bizarre and paradoxical career. It was not, however, and it never will be our idea of what he ought to have done.

Suppose that you or I had been appointed the producers of a messianic final act. Is there any doubt about how we, as the promoters and press agents of a resurrected Savior, would have acted? Of course there isn't. We would have played every card we had to get him on Carson, Donahue, and the cover of *Time*. Or failing that, we would have blitzed local TV and radio with him until the last, least talk-show host lost interest — and then we would have carted him around to county fairs, revival meetings, and supermarket openings till the end of time.

In short, we would have turned the cosmic, risen Jesus — the one who is the Resurrection and the Life of the whole world; the one who, as the creating and redeeming Word of God, is intimately and immediately present to everything that exists; the one who, when he is lifted up, draws *all* to himself; and the one who, at his coming again (his *parousia*), is everywhere at once like lightning that shines from east to west — we would have turned the universal Lord into just another side-show freak. We would have succeeded, to put it succinctly, in convincing the world of our belief that his power lay chiefly in our publicity of him and that his promises — since we gave people no reason to expect anything but right-handed and therefore illusory fulfillments — were just so much hot air.

I realize that the last paragraph was neither "short" nor particularly succinct, but bear with me. The New Testament proclaims an unlikely Savior. The work of Jesus in his incarnation, life, passion, death, resurrection, and ascension makes no worldly sense at all. The portrait the Gospels paint is that of a lifeguard who leaps into the surf, swims to the drowning girl, and then, instead of doing a cross-chest carry, drowns with her, revives three days later, and walks off the beach with assurances that everything, including the apparently still-dead girl, is hunky-dory. You do not like that? Neither do I. But I submit that it is — unless we are prepared to ignore both the Gospels and the ensuing two thousand years' worth of tombstones with bodies still under them — very much like what the Man actually said and did. And — to come to the main point at last — it is the Ascension of Jesus, and the Ascension alone, that keeps us from missing the reason for his doing it that way.

For by ascending, by making a *departure* from this world the capstone of all his earthly acts, he underscores once and for all what he said with ever-increasing clarity through his whole ministry. The kingdom of God, the Ascension insists, does not come about because of what the world does to itself — nor even, in any obvious sense, because of what God does to the world. Rather, the kingdom already exists in the King himself, and when he ascends, the whole world goes with him (John 12:32).

It is not that someday Jesus will do this, that, and the other thing, and then the Kingdom will come. It is not, for example, that *at some future date* the dead will rise or that *in some distant consummation* we will reign with him. Rather, it is that we have already been buried with him in baptism, and that we are already risen with him through faith in the operation of God who raised him from the dead, and that we are now — in this and every moment — enthroned together in heavenly places in Christ Jesus.

But there is more. It is not that, after some further series of transactions, the city — so long mired in sin and failure — will finally be built. Rather, it is that the city, like the kingdom, is already an accomplished fact in Jesus himself. We are invited not to make it happen, but to believe that it *is* and to let it come. It exists, in other words, because in Jesus the world is already the Bride adorned for her husband, because we now sit as his wife at the marriage supper of the Lamb — because, once and for all, *now* and not *then,* he has taken the drowned girl home in the mystery of his death, resurrection, and ascension, and presented her to his Father as the Holy City, the New Jerusalem.

I am aware that many Christians, when they read the passages and images I have just referred to, give them an exclusively future interpretation. But in light of the Ascension, it seems to me, that simply will not wash. Jesus says he *is,* not *will be,* the Way, the Truth, and the Life. He insists to Martha — who quite plausibly figured that her brother Lazarus would rise again at the last day — that he, the Christ himself, is the Resurrection and the Life right now. And he raises Lazarus then and there to drive the point home.

Throughout his ministry, Jesus points relentlessly to himself ("believe in *me*") as the mysterious center from which and in which the Father reconciles the world to himself. Therefore, when he ascends — when he goes away, promising an imminent return — what can that mean but that he has the city fully in hand and ready to be delivered? He always had the whole world in his arms; what the Ascension uniquely proclaims is that he's got the kingdom in his pocket.

To be sure, at the point of his departure, he has it in a highly mysterious pocket: as far as we're concerned we will not see it openly until the delivery is actually made. But that is not because sometime between his Ascension and his Second Coming he will have gotten down to brass tacks and made real what was only virtual. It is only because we can't see mysteries. On the last day, Jesus will not do anything new; he will simply make manifest what he has been doing all along — what, in fact, he has long since done by preparing for us a kingdom from the foundation of the world. It will be in seeing him, as *he* is, that it will finally dawn on us what, in him, we have always been.

In any case, what clinches the argument that the Ascension is the proclamation of a mysterious, left-handed kingdom (already actual in the King himself) is the fact that Jesus discourages any speculation about why he is going or what plans he might have for coming back. The apostles are specifically told that times, seasons, and schedules of events are none of their business. Their relationship to the mystery of the kingdom is to be based not on their knowledge or performance, and certainly not on their guesswork about God's plans; it is to be rooted only in trust in his promise. They are to believe only in the King. Everything else is out of their hands, beyond their ken, and both literally and parabolically, over their heads.

Indeed, it seems to me that the precise reason the early church did not fall apart when Jesus failed to return with any reasonable promptness was that they saw both the Ascension and the Second Coming chiefly as matters of promise. True enough, a certain amount of eschatological explicitness shows up here and there in the records we have (e.g., 1 Thess. 4:13–5:11); but the contexts are often pastoral, and the details vouchsafed are quite plainly put second (as in the passaage cited) to that trust in Jesus that is the one foundation of the church's hope. It was not right-handed, intelligible timetables that kept the first Christians strong in the Lord and armed to resist the methods of the devil — such straight-line plausibilities are just the devil's cup of tea, spoons not long enough by half for anyone to risk supping with him. No, their faithfulness to the kingdom that comes rested solely on the left-handed promise of the King himself. No questions asked; no answers given; just "Amen, come, Lord Jesus."

And what a comfort that is to us, both theologically and pastorally. Not a single specific prediction over the past two millennia has ever come true, but that makes no difference at all. A promise is a promise: whether its fulfillment takes ten seconds or ten billion years, the simple act of trusting it puts us fully, if mysteriously, in the very center of its power.

There is only one thing to add. When Jesus ascended, he not only said he would return; he also promised to endue his church with power from on high (Luke 24:49) — to send them, as he said in John, the Comforter, the Holy Spirit. Interestingly and happily enough, that promise was fulfilled with considerable promptness. The delivery date on it was Pentecost, less than two weeks later. Equally interestingly, but not nearly so happily, the church has made almost as many mistakes about the role of the Spirit in its life as it has about the Second Coming. In spite of the fact that Jesus insisted that the Comforter would not speak of himself but would simply take what was Christ's and show it to us, Christians have all too often decided that there was indeed one thing of Christ's that the Spirit would not bother to show us — one whole set of things, in fact, that Jesus stressed but that the Comforter would not bring to our remembrance — namely, Christ's insistence on using left-handed power.

The idea quickly got around in the early church — and has stayed with us to this day — that when the Spirit came to act, he would do so in plausible, right-handed ways. Whether those acts were conceived of as involving a program of miraculous, healing interventions in the world, or as displaying various straight-line "spiritual" phenomena such as speaking in tongues or guaranteeing the Papacy's infallibility in matters of faith and morals, the church all too often gave the impression that the Spirit could be counted on to deliver in a way that Jesus never did. And thus the mischief was done. The mystery of a kingdom fully accomplished in the risen and ascended King was replaced by a vision of a kingdom to be accomplished by a series of intelligible, selective patch jobs. The Good News of a city founded on grace for everybody became the bad news of a suburb for spiritual millionaires. Jesus said, loud and clear, "I, if I be lifted up, will draw *all* to myself"; the church, louder and clearer, insisted he only meant *some*.

The sad part of it all is that if the world could have been saved by that kind of relatively minor meddling, it would have been — long before Jesus and a hundred times since. But spiritual works no more bring in the kingdom than moral or intellectual ones. The death, resurrection, and ascension of Jesus — especially the Ascension, since it is the final affirmation of the hands-off policy implicit in the other two — proclaim that *no* meddling, divine or human, spiritual or material, can save the world. Its only salvation is in the mystery of the King who dies, rises, and disappears, and who asks us simply to trust his promise that, in him, we have the kingdom already.

THE PARABLES
OF THE KINGDOM

CHAPTER FOUR

The Ministry before the Parables

So far we have dealt with the scriptural framework surrounding the parables and with some of the theological concepts, apt and less apt, by which Christians attempt to grasp it. But if I assess your mood correctly, you have had your fill of talk about the frame and would dearly like to look at the picture. Fair enough. On with the first of the three groupings I originally proposed: Jesus' parables of the kingdom.

By way of a graphic reminder of the general shape of the Gospels, I have included a chart giving the chapter numbers of some of the events of Jesus' ministry that seem to me to bear on the interpretation of the parables. Perhaps the only thing that needs to be said here is that the *parables of the kingdom,* as I see them, occur between columns II and IV of the chart; the *parables of grace,* between columns IV and X; and the *parables of judgment,* between columns X and XI. That much noted, we're ready to proceed.

Chapter Numbers of Some Pivotal Events in the Gospels

Gospel	Total No. of Chaps.	I Jesus' Baptism	II Jesus' Temptation	III The Parable of the Sower	IV The Feeding of the 5,000	V Peter's Confession	VI Jesus' First Prophecy of His Death	VII The Transfiguration	VIII Jesus' Second Prophecy of His Death	IX Jesus' Third Prophecy of His Death	X Palm Sunday	XI Jesus' Death	XII Jesus' Resurrection	XIII Jesus' Ascension
Matt	28	3	4	13	14	16	16	17	17	20	21	27	28	(28)
Mark	16	1	1	4	6	8	8	9	9	10	11	15	16	(16)
Luke	24	3	4	8	9	9	9	9	9	18	19	23	24	24 (+Acts 1)
John	21	—	—	—	6	—	—	—	—	—	12	19	20	—

Since context is crucial, however, we need to begin our consideration of the parables of the kingdom a bit before their appearance in the narration. And since the Gospel according to Mark presents the early events of Jesus' ministry more succinctly than either Matthew or Luke, I propose to limit my examination of those events to the Marcan account.

What do we find in Mark between chapters 1 and 4? Predictably enough, we find Jesus at the very beginning of his public ministry. But what kind of ministry did he seem to be offering to those who heard and saw him? My own answer is that for all concerned, enthusiasts and critics alike, it was an odd and troubling one. And even though its peculiarities, as Mark presents them, succeed one another with such speed and apparent randomness that they are easy to miss, I think that they can be made at least a bit more evident by classifying them under the headings of four tendencies.

First and foremost, Jesus seems quite clearly to be claiming a messianic role for himself. Yet his claim seems also to involve a certain unmessianic flouting of the very Law that his Jewish hearers expected the Messiah to fulfill to perfection. Second — and quite perversely for someone engaged in self-proclamation — Jesus insists that the exorcisms and healings that manifest his messianic identity be kept as much of a secret as possible. Third, both the style and the substance of what he is proclaiming seem to border on something very like irreligion — or at least on something quite beyond his hearers' concept of religion. And fourth, right from the start he manifests a penchant for bent rather than straight discourse: in the first three chapters of Mark, we find not only that Jesus tells parables (3:23), but that he resorts to parabolic sayings no fewer than seven times. Consider, therefore, these four tendencies in order.

As far as the first is concerned, Jesus begins almost immediately to encourage the messianic expectations of the people. As early as Mark 1:15 — a mere two verses after the Temptation — words about the kingdom are already on his lips. "The *time* is here," he says (the Greek word is *kairós,* "due season" — a word with definitely messianic overtones), "and the kingdom of God has drawn close; repent and believe the Good News." But then two verses later, when he sees Simon and Andrew fishing, he says to them, "Come with *me* and *I* will make you fishers of men." Unlike John the Baptist — indeed, unlike most other religious figures — he points toward, not away, from himself when he proclaims his message. And later on, in 2:10 and 2:28, he refers to himself in presumably messianic terms as the Son of Man.

There is more in the same vein. People are amazed at the way he speaks (1:22): unlike the scribes, he teaches with "authority" (*exousía,* power), as if what he says is validated only by his saying it and not by external criteria. Again, he casts out an unclean spirit (1:25) by the same *exousía.* The people are so amazed at his personal authority, in fact, that they wonder whether he is putting forth some totally new teaching. And he continues, doing obviously messianic signs (the healing of Simon's mother-in-law [1:30]; the healing of many sick people and the driving out of many demons [1:34, 39]; the cleansing of a leper [1:40]; the healing of a paralytic [2:3]).

But he then proceeds to associate with sleazy types that no proper Messiah would have any truck with. In 2:14, he calls Levi, a tax-farmer, to follow him (in his audience's mind, a good tax collector was simply a contradiction in terms — rather like a poverty-stricken dermatologist in our day and age). He follows that up by eating dinner with a whole crowd of tax collectors and low-lifes (2:15), and when some Pharisees question the appropriateness of the company he keeps (2:16), he justifies himself by saying that it is precisely sinners, and not the righteous, that he has come to call. It's worth noting, too, that neither in this last passage nor in the parallel account in Matthew 9:13 does Jesus say anything more than that he has "come to *call* sinners." He does not add "to repentance" as he does in Luke 5:32; he just insists that his call is to the disreputable rather than to the upright — an insistence that, to the Pharisees who were its target, could only mean that Jesus, for all his messianic pretensions, had a strange lack of interest in looking like a respectable Messiah.

Finally (to complete this first heading), Jesus flies still further in the face of messianic expectations. He justifies the apparent irreligiousness of his disciples' failure to fast by asking, "Who can avoid being at a party when I'm around?" (2:19). He says that old notions about the Messiah are totally inappropriate to his new and definitive messiahship (2:21). And he violates the Sabbath not once, but twice: by picking grain (2:23) and by healing a man with a withered hand (3:1). After the first of those violations, he justifies himself by saying that he, the Son of Man, is in charge of the Sabbath, not the other way around. And after the second, the Pharisees have heard all they need to convince them that Jesus is unqualified bad news: as early as Mark 3:6, plans to kill Jesus are already afoot.

In other words, by the time Mark reaches chapter 4 and introduces the parable of the Sower (the first of the explicit parables of the messianic kingdom), he has already established Jesus not only as a wonder-working, demon-exorcising claimant to the messianic title but also as a Sabbath-breaking upstart with a dangerously arrogant sense of his own authority — as somebody, in other words, who is neither interested in, nor palatable to, the religious sensibilities of expert Messiah-watchers. To sum it up, therefore: by the end of chapter 3, his family thinks he is crazy (v. 21); the scribes are sure he is possessed by Beelzebub (v. 22); and Jesus' patience is already beginning to wear thin. The Satan-talk, he insists, is sheer nonsense (vv. 23-29); his real family consists of anybody who does the will of God (v. 35); and those who say he has an evil spirit are themselves guilty of blaspheming against the Holy Spirit (vv. 29-30).

My second heading — the matter of the "messianic secret" — can be dealt with more briefly. Let it simply be read into the record here that in at least three places (Mark 1:34, 44; and 3:12) Jesus, who is obviously in the process of putting himself forth as a messianic figure, paradoxically charges those who have the most proof of his messiahship not to utter a word about it. On the first occasion he will not let the demons he has driven out speak; on the second, he tells a cleansed leper not to say anything to anybody; and on the third, he extensively warns the unclean spirits not to blow his cover. Why? Mark does not say. Perhaps it was because Jesus saw clearly, right from the start (he certainly said as much soon after this in 4:12), that any Messiah his hearers would recognize would not be the kind of Messiah he was. Or perhaps it was just because he felt he did not want to give hostile critics more ammunition than they already had.

In any case, the facts stand: Jesus not only revealed himself, he hid himself at the same time. It was a pattern, it seems to me, that eventually became a passion with him. Whatever we make of it, there is no question but that right up to his seemingly inconsequential death, his elusive resurrection, and his uncommunicative ascension — indeed, with ever-increasing clarity through all three of those climactic events — he went right on doing the same thing: reconciling the world by a kind of divine double-talk, proclaiming approach-avoidance as the paradigm of salvation.

The third heading — the apparent "irreligiousness" of Jesus' early words and acts — needs even less space, since some instances of it have already been mentioned. I add here only that, to judge from the responses Jesus provoked from the religious experts of his day, it is quite plain that what he said and did didn't look much like religion to them. Respectable religionists can spot an absence of conventional piety a mile away; and the scribes and Pharisees did just that. In Mark 2:6, 16, 18, 24, and 3:2, they're increasingly sure there is something about Jesus' message that they want no part of. By 3:6 their certainty has been extended to not wanting any part of Jesus himself either, and to actually making plans to kill him. And by 3:22 they have their case complete. Not only is he an irreligious and therefore bogus messiah who should be killed as soon as possible; he is also the exact opposite of the Messiah: he is, they are convinced, the devil incarnate.

On then to the last of the four tendencies in the early chapters of Mark: the fact that Jesus speaks parabolically even before he begins uttering the parables we recognize as such. I shall do no more than list the instances. If they are not quite up to the standards of some of his later performances, neither were all of his later performances. The acted parables of the Cursing of the Fig Tree, for instance, or of the Coin in the Fish's Mouth, do not seem of as great a stature as, say, the Prodigal Son or the Unforgiving Servant. Jesus had better and worse days, I suppose, just like everyone else. In any case, they show quite clearly that from the outset, he habitually thought in terms of comparisons and that, whenever he spotted an opening for it, he liked nothing better than to speak about two subjects at the same time.

Here, then, are the "parables before the parables" as they appear in Mark: "I will make you fishers of men" (1:17). "Those who are well do not need a doctor, only those who are sick" (2:17). "Are the wedding guests able to fast while the bridegroom is still with them?" (2:19). "Nobody puts new wine into old wineskins" (2:22). "If a kingdom be divided against itself, it is not possible for that kingdom to stand" (3:24). "If a house be divided against itself, that house will not be able to stand" (3:25). "He looked over the people who were sitting around him and said, 'Look, here are my mother and my brothers'" (3:34).

As I said — and as the chart at the beginning of this chapter makes clear — Matthew and Luke take longer to cover the preliminary ground that Mark traverses in three chapters. They also, of course, include additional material — most notably, perhaps, the "Sermon on the Mount" (or "in the Plain"). But since they omit very little of the Marcan account, the summary given here of the early events of Jesus' ministry is reasonably adequate for them as well. True enough, the other two synoptic Gospels may seem to take some of the "edge" off the story. Many of the passages they add display a Jesus who seems to be a shade less at odds with the authorities than the one portrayed by Mark; events in Matthew and Luke move at a more leisurely pace.

Still, it is fair to say that when all three of the synoptic Gospels arrive at the point where the parables of the kingdom begin (Matt. 13; Mark 4; Luke 8), they are in substantial agreement: they show us Jesus as a Messiah who already fits no known messianic mold, and they set the stage for the utter breaking of the mold that is about to begin.

CHAPTER FIVE

The Sower: The Watershed of the Parables

By far the largest concentration of the parables of the kingdom occurs in the Gospel of Matthew. Using chapter 13 of Matthew as the principal source, therefore — and simply noting where duplications, omissions, or additions occur in Mark and Luke — we come up with the following list:

Matthew	Name of Parable or Passage	Mark	Luke
13:1-9	The Sower	4:1-9	8:4-8
13:10-17	The purpose of parables	4:10-12	8:9-10
13:18-23	Interpretation of the Sower	4:13-20	8:11-15
5:15	The Lamp	4:21-25	8:16-18
(missing)	The Growing Seed	4:26-29	(missing)
13:24-30	The Weeds	(missing)	(missing)
13:31-32	The Mustard Seed	4:30-32	13:18-19
13:33	The Leaven	(missing)	13:20-21
13:34-35	Jesus says nothing without a parable	4:33-34	(missing)
13:36-43	Interpretation of the Weeds	(missing)	(missing)
13:44	The Treasure Hidden in a Field	(missing)	(missing)
13:45-46	The Pearl of Great Price	(missing)	(missing)
13:47-50	The Net	(missing)	(missing)
13:51-52	The Householder	(missing)	(missing)

The first thing to note about this list is the star billing that the synoptic Gospels give to the parable of the Sower. Not only do all three of them make it the introduction to the first deliberate collection of Jesus' parables; they also devote a disproportionate amount of space to it and to the comments Jesus made in connection with it. For the record, Matthew gives this material twenty-three verses; Mark, twenty-five; and Luke, fifteen. It is well known that a number of biblical critics have found fault with the Sower, and particularly with Jesus' allegorized interpretation of it. It is, they claim, less than a parable in the true sense of the word. The synoptic Gospel writers themselves, however, apparently found nothing deficient about it; and their unanimity in using it as a preface to Jesus' parables strikes me as far more significant than any critical nit-picking. Indeed, I think that in the minds of careful Bible readers, a flag should go up every time the Gospels give such across-the-board treatment to anything.

To take but two other instances (leaving aside such major items as the Triumphal Entry, the Cleansing of the Temple, the Last Supper, the Crucifixion, and the Resurrection), consider the Feeding of the Five Thousand and the Transfiguration. It seems to me that in each case the writers have a clear sense that they are dealing with a major turning point in Jesus' history. Something that heretofore was only (or barely) hinted at is about to be made manifest. Pressures that were scarcely felt are shortly to be given another turn of the developmental screw.

The Feeding of the Five Thousand, as I already noted, is the preface to a fairly explicit shift in Jesus' mind toward left-handed rather than right-handed uses of power. And the Transfiguration (along with Peter's confession, which serves as a prologue to it) is even more clearly presented as a turning point. Prior to it, the synoptics show us a fairly upbeat Jesus who, for all his mysteriousness, can still be taken as a standard-issue, wonder-working Messiah. But after the Transfiguration the story becomes dark and brooding. Jesus says in so many words that his messiahship will inevitably involve death and resurrection; the certainty of that terrible "exodus" of his (as Luke calls it) colors all his subsequent sayings and actions.

The parable of the Sower, therefore, seems to be yet another of the Gospel "flags." Take, for example, the matter of the "messianic secret." Prior to the Sower, Jesus' reluctance to come right out and declare his messiahship in plain terms was mostly a matter of occasional warnings — both to demons and to the beneficiaries of his signs — not to reveal who he really was. Subsequently, though, it becomes a kind of intentional mystification that he incorporates into his teaching as a deliberate principle. To see that, all you have to do is note the words of Isaiah that Jesus interposes between the Sower and its interpretation: He says that he speaks to the people in parables in order that "seeing they might not see and hearing they might not understand." Till now, in other words, he has been aware in a general way that his kind of messiahship is not what people have been expecting; but from here on he takes this preliminary, mostly negative perception and turns it into a positive developmental principle of his thinking. "Well," he seems to say, "since they've pretty well misunderstood me so far, maybe I should capitalize on that. Maybe I should start thinking up examples of how profoundly the true messianic kingdom differs from their expectations. They think the kingdom will be a parochial, visible proposition — a militarily established theocratic state that will simply be handed to them at some future date. H'm. What if I were to stand every one of those ideas on its head? What if I were to come up with some parables that said the kingdom was catholic, mysterious, already present in their midst, and aggressively demanding their response? Let me see. . . ."

Whatever his thoughts, their outcome was what we have in Matthew 13 and its parallels: the proclamation of exactly such a paradoxical kingdom. Furthermore, these passages show Jesus giving not only a new substance but also a new style to his proclamation — a style that will turn out to be the most important single development in his teaching technique. For the first time (in the Sower and the Weeds), he goes beyond mere comparisons and produces parables that are actually stories.

Admittedly, by comparison with his later refinements of the technique, these early narrative parables may seem a bit thin. But then, early Mozart and early Beethoven are open to the same criticism. What needs to be said for Jesus — and for all other great artists — is that such comparisons are largely irrelevant. The early productions of the masters are marvels in and of themselves; whatever else might be said about them, they are, in retrospect, exactly what seems to have been called for at the point where they appeared. The rest of the *oeuvre* occurred not only after them but also, in some important sense, because of them. Therefore, the parable of the Sower stands quite easily as what the synoptics make it: the great watershed of all Jesus' parables.

Turning to the parable itself, then, the first thing to note is its three-step presentation by the synoptics. Each of them begins with the parable itself, unadorned by any commentary. Then comes a section in which the disciples ask Jesus a question. In Matthew and Mark, they inquire in a general sort of way why he uses parables when he speaks to the people; in Luke, the question is specifically about the meaning of the parable of the Sower. Finally, all three Gospel writers conclude their accounts with Jesus' own allegorical interpretation of the parable.

This three-step sequence, I think, is crucial to an understanding of the Sower. Not only should we take it seriously as the order in which Jesus put forth this material; we should also make a special effort to avoid a common Christian presumption about it. As a result of two thousand years of familiarity, we find it oddly redundant. We assume all too easily that the disciples must have been particularly dense to have had so much trouble understanding such a simple story. To us, the parable seems obvious quite on its own; the interpretation sounds like nothing so much as a belaboring of the obvious. In particular, we are at a loss to explain the insertion, between the two, of the passage about Jesus' reason for speaking in parables. The truth of the matter, however, is that if we had been the original hearers, we would probably have understood it no better than the disciples did. As proof, consider the fact that we quite regularly miss its meaning even now.

Despite what we may think, the parable as Jesus first gives it is not at all obvious to people hearing it for the first time. For one thing, he does not say what it is that he's talking about; he simply launches into a seemingly straightforward story about a farmer whose scattered seed falls into four different situations: some on the road, some on rocky ground, some among thorns, and some on good ground. Obviously, he is talking about something besides agriculture; but as to what that other subject might be, he gives not a single clue. It seems to me that if we are honest with ourselves, we would have come up with exactly the same questions as the disciples. We, right along with them, would have asked either, "Why are you talking in riddles like that?" or, "What on earth is the meaning of what you just said?"

Obligingly, Jesus tells them what the other subject is: the kingdom. (In Matthew, he calls it "the kingdom of the heavens"; in Mark and Luke, "the kingdom of God" — but the phrases are otherwise equivalent.) "To you," he tells the disciples, "it has been given to know the secrets [*ta mystéria* — the hidden things, the unobservable workings] of the kingdom, but for those outside, it is given only in parables."

Then follow two startling statements. The first is "for to him who has, more will be given; and from him who has not, even what he has will be taken away." This seems to me to be one of those hard sayings of Jesus that cries out, not for a prescriptive interpretation, but for a descriptive one. Jesus, though he could be taken as issuing a statement about what God will do to reward or punish those who hear the parables, seems to be more reasonably understood as giving a simple description of the way things are. "If you grasp the fact that the kingdom works in a mystery," he seems to say, "then that very grip will give you more and more understanding; but if you don't grasp that, then everything that happens will make it look as if your plausibility-loving understanding is being deliberately taken from you."

Jesus made such descriptive comments at other times: for example, in Mark 10:23, his "How hard it is for those who have possessions to enter into the kingdom of God" seems more a lament at the way riches get in people's way than a statement that God is going to put obstacles in front of them just because they are rich. At any rate, in this case the descriptive interpretation is the one borne out by the Gospel history: those who had a grip, by faith, on the fact that the mystery was ultimately *Jesus himself* were able to find the Crucifixion/Resurrection the source of ever greater understanding; those who didn't, on the other hand, found it nothing but a colossal unintelligibility.

The second startling statement is another hard saying that likewise makes little sense if given a simplistic, prescriptive interpretation. Jesus justifies his use of parables by quoting Isaiah: "So that they may look and look, yet not see, and listen and listen, yet not understand . . . lest they should turn again and be forgiven." Once again, this is not the announcement of a divine double-cross by which God is going to trick people into a situation where he can finally zap them with condemnation instead of forgiveness (a notion, incidentally, that goes clean against the heart of the Gospel). Rather, it is another one of those sad, head-shaking reflections on the way things are. Jesus thinks about the obtuseness he sees all around him — about the unlikelihood of anybody's getting even a glimmer of the mystery, let alone a grip on it — and the passage from Scripture pops into his mind as the perfect summary: "Isaiah really had it right," he thinks, and then he simply recites the verses out loud.

"But," you wonder, "what about the fact that Jesus then proceeds to interpret the parable of the Sower? Doesn't spelling it out for them like that indicate he really does want them to understand after all?"

There are two ways of answering that. The first is to make a distinction: Jesus gave the *disciples* the interpretation, but left those outside in the dark. On that basis, the proper interpretation seems to be that he was giving the disciples, who already had at least a clue, a bit of the "more" he had spoken of a minute earlier; and by not explaining it to the masses, he was taking away even what they had. But that seems to me a poor answer. For one thing, the disciples don't seem — at least until after the Crucifixion/Resurrection — to have had noticeably more understanding than anybody else. For another, while the masses may not have been given the interpretation the first time around, the fact that the Gospel writers included it in the account guaranteed that they would have it forever after. Therefore, the crux of the interpretation should not be made to lie in the matter of who was given an explanation and who wasn't; rather, it should rest on what Jesus was up to in giving the explanation at all.

That brings us to the second and better way of looking at the passage. To be sure, the usual view of the parable of the Sower is that Jesus, when he allegorizes it for the disciples (Matt. 13:18-23 and parallels), is taking the dark, unintelligible parable he first told and somehow making it simpler and more accessible to their minds (in spite of the fact, please note, that he has just gotten through saying that that is not at all what he intends, at least not for those outside). But such a view has one whopping flaw: the "explanation" of the parable does not in fact make it easier to understand; instead, coming as it does after the flat statement (Matt. 13:11 and parallels) that Jesus is talking about the kingdom, it presents even the disciples' minds with a whole raft of ideas that are harder still to digest.

Jesus' explanation of the Sower, if it is looked at with an open mind, does not reduce what was a complex story to a simple meaning; rather, it takes a merely puzzling fable and drives it for all it's worth in the direction of supremely difficult interpretations. By insisting as it does on what I have referred to as the kingdom's notes of *catholicity, mystery,* and *present actuality* — and by presenting the kingdom as calling for a *response* in the midst of a largely *hostile* world — it causes the lights in the minds of all Jesus' hearers to go out, not on.

Even in ours. For example, take only the very beginning of the explanation. In Mark and Luke (though not in Matthew) Jesus says (if I may conflate the texts) that the sower sows the Word of God. What do we make of that? Do we "get" it? Do we act as a church in a way that takes such an assertion seriously? I submit that we do not.

Whom do we usually identify as the sower? We think it's Jesus, don't we? And we have in our minds an image of him — and then of ourselves as the church — going around sprinkling something called the Word of God on places that haven't yet received it. But that, on any fair reading of Jesus' words, makes no sense at all. The primary meaning of the phrase the *Word of God* in the New Testament, and in Christian theology as well, has got to be one that is consistent with the Johannine teaching that the Word is the one who was in the beginning with God and who is, in fact, God himself. More than that, it has to include the notions that the Word is the one by whom all things were made, that he is the one who, coming into the world, lightens every person, and that he is the one, finally, who became flesh and dwelt among us in Jesus. In short, and above everything else, *the Word* has to mean the eternal Son — God of God, Light of Light, True God of True God — the Second Person of the Holy and Undivided Trinity.

Do you see what that says? It says, first of all, that the Sower is God the Father, not Jesus. What Jesus turns out to be — since he is the Word — is the seed sown. But note what that in turn means. It means that on the plain terms of the parable, Jesus has already, and literally, been sown everywhere in the world — and quite without a single bit of earthly cooperation or even consent. But can you tell me that Christians in general have ever for long acted as if that were the case? Have we not acted instead as if the Word wasn't anywhere until we got there with him? Haven't we conducted far too many missions on the assumption that we were "bringing Jesus" to the heathen, when in fact all we had to bring was the Good News of what the Word — who was already there — had done for them? Haven't we, in short, ended up just as he said we would as a result of his explanation of the Sower? We see and hear and still don't catch on. For twenty centuries we have read that the Word of God is what is sown; yet to judge from the way the church does business most of the time, Jesus might just as well have said that the Word is precisely what is *not* sown.

Therefore, the apparent simplification involved in Jesus' allegorization of the parable of the Sower is nothing of the kind; in fact, his interpretation makes the parable profoundly complex. And we bear witness to that complexity: in these passages, Jesus has kicked the whole mystery of the kingdom so far upstairs that many Christians, for most of the church's history, have missed his point completely and chosen instead to busy themselves with downright contradictions of it. It is time, therefore, to examine the parable in detail — and to note, as we go, how many examples of our inveterate noncomprehension there are in addition to the one just cited.

CHAPTER SIX

The Sower, Continued

One concession. You may feel I have given you a fast shuffle by introducing into the parable of the Sower not only the theology of the Word from John 1 but also the full-blown christology of the Nicene Creed. I grant you that, but with a distinction: if it was a shuffle, it was not an illegitimately fast one.

I do not think, of course, that when Jesus told the parable for the first time he necessarily had any of those later theological formulations in his human mind. For all I know, he may even have thought of himself as the sower, and conceived of the Word sown as little more than the Good News of the kingdom. It probably did not occur to him that he was, in fact, that very Word, and I think it quite certain that the Johannine concepts of the Word as God and the Word as made flesh never entered his head.

And yet. There is no way of completely separating the parable of the Sower from the subsequent developments of its themes in other parables. Indeed, if we believe in the inspiration of Scripture, there is nothing finally desirable about divorcing it from the later contributions of, say, John or Paul or any other New Testament writer. For example, on the presumption that the author of the Fourth Gospel was familiar with the parable of the Sower, it is likely that he was not unaware that his development of the doctrine of the Word as divine would bear directly on the interpretation of the Word as sown. At the very least, the Holy Spirit was definitely aware of it, and as the ultimate genius presiding over the formation of the whole canon of Scripture, the Spirit had no more difficulty working backward than forward. Concepts that he had not fit in by means of an earlier passage, he easily retrofitted, as it were, by means of a later one.

Even if we do no more than confine ourselves to chapter 13 of Matthew, its string of shortish parables of the kingdom develops mightily the mysterious themes sketched in the Sower. If we toss in the parables of grace as well, we find the mystery of the kingdom more and more closely identified with Jesus himself (the parable of the Watchful Servants in Luke 12:35-48). If we include the parables of judgment, we find him saying that the final constitution of the kingdom rests entirely on relationship with him — and on that relationship as operative in the mystery of his catholic presence in all human beings (the parable of the Great Judgment, Matt. 25:31-46). And finally, if we take in the rest of his words and deeds, we find him claiming at the Last Supper that the cup is the New Covenant in his blood (Luke 22:20). In short, we find him asserting that in himself — in his death, resurrection, and ascension — whatever is necessary for the fullness of the kingdom has been accomplished purely and simply by what he has done.

It seems to me, therefore, that the right way to express both the continuity and the development of Jesus' thoughts about the connection between the kingdom and himself is to say that, from the parable of the Sower to the end of the New Testament, we are watching the opening of a bud into full flower. The early stages of the process may not look much like the final result, but if we examine the entire development carefully, we will find that everything in the end is, one way or another, totally consonant with what was there from the beginning. With that interpretive principle in mind, I return to the parable of the Sower itself — and to the headings of *catholicity, mystery, actuality, hostility,* and *response* under which I have proposed to treat it.

Catholicity

The idea of the catholicity of the kingdom — the insistence that it is at work everywhere, always, and for all, rather than in some places, at some times, and for some people — is an integral part of Jesus' teaching from start to finish. True, at the outset of his ministry it is expressed by little more than his irksome tendency to sit loose to the highly parochial messianic notions of his hearers — by, for example, his breaking of the Sabbath, his consorting with undesirable types, and his constant challenging of the narrow views of the scribes and Pharisees. But it becomes practically the hallmark of his teaching once he begins his use of the parabolic method in earnest.

Not only does he resort, as in the parable of the Leaven (Matt. 13:33), to the occasional illustration that quite literally uses the word "whole" (the *hólon* in cat*hol*ic); far more often, he sets up his parables in such a way that by their very terms they cover nothing less than the whole world. The device he uses may not be obvious to the casual reader, but once it has been spotted, it can be seen again and again. When Jesus sketches his parabolic characters or circumstances, he often drafts them so inclusively that no one, at any time or in any place, is left out of the scope of his teaching.

Consider some instances. In the Sower, the four kinds of ground listed are clearly meant to cover all sorts and conditions of human beings; there are no cracks between them into which odd cases might fall, and there is no ground beyond them to which his words do not apply. In the parable of the Weeds he simply says that "the field is the world" (Matt. 13:38). In the Net (Matt. 13:47) he says the kingdom catches *all* kinds. And in his later parables, he develops this technique of including everybody into something close to an art form. Let me give you a handful of random examples. In the parable of the Forgiving Father (Luke 15:11-32), the whole human race's relationship to grace is neatly divided between the prodigal and the elder brother. Likewise, in the story of the Pharisee and the Publican (Luke 18:9-14) there is no one in the world who can't be comprehended under one or the other character. And in the parable of the Feast for the King's Son's Wedding (Matt. 22:1-14), there is not a single kind of response to grace that is left out: the characters in the parable — whether they are graciously invited or compelled to attend, whether they accept or reject the King's party — are plainly intended as stand-ins for the great, gray-green, greasy catholic mass of humanity with which God insists on doing business.

In the case of the parable of the Sower, however, there is still another, if more subtle, indication of the note of catholicity. Jesus' parables, even when they were not spoken to anyone outside the small group of the disciples, were set forth, as I have said, in a context of highly parochial ideas about God's relationship with the world. If you have any feeling for the way narrow minds work, you will realize that the Sower, as told, would immediately strike such minds as reeking of the catholicity they had spent their entire religious lives deploring. People who are that narrow do not really listen to what someone says; rather, they sniff at his words

— they check them over to spot the squishy, rotten spots through which ideas they hate might seep in.

In the case of the Sower, they would have had a field day. First, by making no specific reference to Israel, Jesus feeds their suspicions about his lack of proper parochialism. Of course, the parable could perfectly well be about God's relationship with the Jews alone, but for suspicious minds, *could be* is never an acceptable substitute for *has got to be*. They want an airtight case, not a leaky one; what Jesus gave them has enough holes in it to let in all the Gentiles in the world.

Second, their nervous-nelly fear of a truly catholic kingdom leads them to an even deeper reason for distrust. Not only has Jesus told a story on whose terms the Gentiles might be brought in; worse yet, he has told one that just as plainly gives no guarantee that the chosen people might not be left out. By skirting the whole Jew-Gentile issue, you see, Jesus has, in fact, raised it more strongly than ever in his hearers' minds. What he *says,* they can't very well argue with, but what it *smells like* — ah, *that* they are not about to take sitting down.

Am I putting too much weight on this? I don't think so. At the end of his interpretation of the Sower, Jesus adds a few remarks (Mark 4:21-25 and parallels). All of them, it strikes me, are rather edgy. He does not sound like a cool rabbi who has delivered an unexceptionably pious lesson; instead, he sounds like someone who has just said something he knows is offensive but who is bound and determined to make it stick.

The first remark — "Does anyone ever bring in a lamp and put it under the bed?" — seems to me roughly equivalent to "What am I supposed to do, hide the truth just because people don't like it?" His second — "There is nothing hid, except to be made manifest" — has to have been offensive to those who believed that God had already disclosed, *to them*, everything that really mattered. His third — "He who has ears to hear, let him hear" — sounds like nothing so much as "I dare you to think about all these implications that are terrifying you." His fourth — "Watch how you hear: the way you measure out judgment will be the way it's measured out to you, and even more severely" — practically makes my case all by itself. And his final remark, in which he repeats his preface to the interpretation of the Sower — "To him who has, more will more be given; and from him who has not, even what he has will be taken away" — is entirely too vague about the identity of the several "whos" to be of much comfort to anybody.

But the real clincher of the case for the catholicity of the Sower is the collection of parables following Matthew 13:24-52 (and parallels) that so clearly develops the catholicity of the kingdom. The synoptic writers plainly feel that all this material is of a piece: even if one or the other of the notes I have listed is merely adumbrated in the parable of the Sower, each of them, as the succeeding parables unfold, is given its turn at a full-dress exposition. Therefore, leaving the rest of the subject of catholicity to be treated when we look at those parables individually, I proceed to the next of the notes as it is manifested in the Sower.

Mystery

I have made it clear that I consider Jesus' ever-increasing preference for left-handed rather than right-handed uses of power to be the most significant development of his thinking over the course of his ministry. But it is in the parable of the Sower that he takes the first quiet but major step in the direction that will eventually lead him into the heart of the paradox of power. And not only him. If we pay close attention to the Sower, we, too, will be led the same way: we, too, will come to see the apparent inaction of the Cross, the only minimally noticeable fact of the Resurrection, and the totally disappointing episode of the Ascension as the final flowering of the Good News he proclaimed from the very beginning.

I refer, of course, to his use of the imagery of *seed* and *sowing* as the principal analogue in the parable. To be sure, this is not the only place he refers to them; his use of *spóros* (seed), of *speírein* (to sow), and of *kókkos* (seed, grain) occurs in other passages (Matt. 13:24-27; Matt. 13:31 and parallels; Matt. 17:20 and parallels; and John 12:24). But this is the first and thus the most significant reference from the point of view of development.

Consider the imagery of seed. First of all, seeds are disproportionately small compared with what they eventually produce. In the case of herbs — which, for some reason, Jesus took special delight in — they are in fact almost ridiculously small. Anyone who has planted thyme or savory knows the strange sensation of practically losing sight of the seed after it has been dropped into the furrow: you might as well have sown nothing, for all you can observe. And what does that say about the Word of God that the Sower sows? Well, it certainly does not say what we would have said. Left to our own devices we would probably have likened the Word's advent to a thunderclap, or to a fireworks display, or to something else we judged sufficiently unmistakable to stand in for our notion of a pushy, totally right-handed God. Instead, this parable says that the true coming of the Word of God, even if you see it, doesn't look like very much — and that when it does finally get around to doing its real work, it is so mysterious that it can't even be found at all.

That is the second thing about seeds: they disappear. In the obvious sense, they do so because of their need to be covered over with earth in order to function. (Think of the light that *that* sheds on the "messianic secret": Jesus is taking what may have been only an instinctive dislike for publicity and turning it into a theological principle.) But in the profound sense, they disappear because once they are thus covered, they eventually become not only unrecognizable but undiscoverable as well: as far as their own being is concerned, they simply die and disappear.

Think of what that says about Jesus and how it reechoes through his whole ministry. He, as the Word, comes to his own and his own receive him not. He is despised. He is the stone the builders rejected. He is ministered to, not in his own recognizable form but in the sick, the imprisoned, and the generally down-and-out. And to cap his whole career as the Word sown in the field of the world, he dies, rises, and vanishes. His entire work proceeds as does the work of a seed: it takes place in a mystery, in secret — in a way that, as Luther said, can neither be known nor felt, but only *believed, trusted.*

Once again, that is not our idea of how a respectable divine operation ought to be run. We would rather have causalities and agencies that were a bit more proportionate to their results. Given our druthers, our pet illustration of the kingdom would probably be a giant nail — driven into the world, appropriately enough, by a giant hammer in the hand of a giant God. Something noisy and noticeable. But a seed? Oh, come now.

Actuality

If we have difficulty adjusting to a Word of God who works as minimally and mysteriously as a seed, we will have even more difficulty with the next point to be made about seeds, namely, that they actually do work. The sower in the parable is depicted in the act of sowing. He is not sitting in his armchair reading seed catalogs in February; he is not tilling and fertilizing the soil in March; and above all, he is not standing in the garden in May, simply thinking about taking the seeds out of their packages. If he were shown doing any of those things, we might fairly conclude that the power of the Word — like the power of seeds under similar circumstances — was only *virtually* present in the world. We might assume, in other words, that it would not achieve *actual* effectiveness until some further steps were taken.

In the terms of the parable as told, however, there is no room for such virtualism. The seed, and therefore the Word, is fully in action in and of itself at every step of the story. Everything necessary for its perfect work is *in the works* from the start. Even the apparent contradictions of its effectiveness that appear in the course of the parable turn out not to deny that effectiveness at all.

First, consider the seed that falls on the road and is eaten by birds. That is no denial of its properties as seed. Seeds, from an ecological point of view, have purposes other than the reproduction of species: they are attractive to birds; they are nourishing to almost all animals; and they are quite literally the spice of human life. To be sure, Jesus equates the birds with the devil. But the comparison, while perhaps hard on the birds, is by no means unflattering either way. The demons knew who Jesus was even when people didn't. Therefore, just as the birds recognize seed for what it is even if the pavement doesn't, so the devil recognizes the power of the Word even when human beings don't. Furthermore, just as the effective power of seeds to reproduce themselves is in no way seriously inhibited by the depredations of the birds (in fact, animal ingestion and excretion of seeds is one of nature's ways of insuring their distribution), so too the effective power of the Word is not lessened even though the devil may try to digest it for his own purposes and turn it into offal. The Word, like the seed, still works on its own terms.

Next, however, consider the seed that falls into the other three situations. In all of them — whether on the rocky ground, in the thorny underbrush, or in the well-prepared soil — the seed actually does its proper, reproductive work: it springs up. True, there are differences in the outcome of that work, and I shall have something to say about them by and by. But what needs to be emphasized here is that the differences can never be interpreted as meaning that the operative power of the seed — or the operative power of the Word — is in any way dependent on circumstantial cooperation.

Perversely, though, we seem to prefer that interpretation. The history of Christian thought is riddled with virtualism. "Sure," we have said, "the Lamb of God has taken away all the sins of the world." But then we have proceeded to give the impression that unless people did something special to activate it, his forgiveness would remain only virtually, not actually, theirs. Think of some of the things we have said to people. We have told them that unless they confessed to a priest, or had the sacrifice of the mass applied specifically to their case, or accepted Jesus in the correct denominational terms — or hit the sawdust trail, did penance, cried their eyes out, or straightened up and flew right — the seed, who is the Word present everywhere in all his forgiving power, might just as well not really have been sown.

Once again, this note of power *actually present* — this flat precluding of even a hint of virtualism in the proclamation of the Gospel — comes through even more clearly in the rest of the parables of the kingdom, especially when they involve, as they do here, the imagery of seeds. Before coming to those, however, let me end this consideration of the Sower by dealing with my last two headings at the same time.

Hostility and Response

The idea that the Good News of the kingdom is proclaimed in a hostile environment is written all over the New Testament. Whether we look at the demons who recognize Jesus or at the religious establishment that refuses to, it is quite plain that antagonism is every bit as much the soil of the Word as is acceptance. The point is, literally, crucial: the supreme act by which the Word declares the kingdom in all its power is not an act at all but a death on the cross inflicted on him by his enemies. Therefore, whatever else needs to be said about hostility to the Word — about its power and function in the Gospels or about the presumed menace it poses in our own day — the first thing to be insisted on is that all the antagonism in the world has already been aced out by Jesus. Not overcome by force as we would have done — not bludgeoned into submission or out of existence — but precisely *aced out:* finessed, tricked into doing God's thing when all the while it thought it was doing its own thing.

Consider the devil first. Christians have spent too much time in one or the other of two pointless pursuits. Either they have denied the reality of praeter-human evil, or they have given the Old Deceiver far more time and attention than he deserves. This is no place to settle the question of the existence of Satan and his henchmen, so, along with Scripture, I shall simply assume it. But this is also no place to get upset about it, to act as if the hosts of evil were not already, in the mystery of his death and resurrection, beaten by Jesus. Like the birds that nibble on the seeds and then pass them out of their bodies unimpaired, the devil has no power against the Word. Whatever warfare might have been necessary against him has already been undertaken and won. "My sheep hear my voice," Jesus says, "and I give them eternal life, . . . they shall never perish, and no one shall pluck them out of my hand" (John 10:27-28).

Nobody, in other words — not the devil, not the world, not the flesh, not even ourselves — can take us away from the Love that will not let us go. We can, of course, squirm in his grip and despise his holding of us, and we can no doubt get ourselves into one hell of a mess by doing so. But if he is God the Word who both makes and reconciles us, there is no way — no way, literally, even in hell — that we will ever find ourselves anywhere else than in the very thick of both our creation and our reconciliation. All the evil in the universe, whether from the devil or from us, is now and ever shall be just part of the divine ecology.

And the Sower says that. The seed eaten by birds is as much seed as the seed that produced a hundredfold. The snatching of the Word by the devil — and the rejection of it by the shallow and the choking of it by the worldly — all take place *within* the working of the kingdom, not prior to it or outside of it. It is the Word alone, and not the interference with it, that finally counts. True enough, and fittingly enough, the most obvious point in the whole parable is that the fullest enjoyment of the fruitfulness of the Word is available only to those who interfere with it least. But even in making that point, Jesus still hammers away at the sovereignty and sole effectiveness of the Word. Those on the good ground, he says, are those who simply hear the Word, accept it, and bear fruit: some thirty-, some sixty-, and some a hundredfold. It's not that they *do* anything, you see; rather, it's that they *don't* do things that get in the Word's way. It's the Word, and the Word alone, that does all the rest.

One note in passing: In our day and age, we have come to understand that seeds don't do all the work — that the environment, materially speaking, contributes almost one hundred percent of what is contained in the full-grown, fructifying plant. But in Jesus' day, and for a very long time after it, that was not the common supposition. However much we might be tempted to drag human contributions into our interpretation of the parable, therefore, the story *as told* rests squarely on the sole agency of both the seed and the Word.

Nevertheless, it remains true that *response* to the sowing of the Word is made the final thrust of the parable (though even at that, the thirty-, sixty-, one hundredfold yield — based on no apparent differences in the good ground — is tossed in as a further indication of both the Word's power and its mysterious sovereignty over the whole process). In speaking about response, however, we need to take note of a peculiarity in Jesus' explanation of the parable. He clearly says that the seed sown is the Word of God. But when he comes to the results of the sowing, he is a bit more vague: he refers to those who respond as "the ones along the road," or as "what was sown among thorns," or as "those sown upon the good ground," and so on (Mark 4:15-20).

At first blush, these phrases seem to refer to the seed; but unless we want to welsh on the identity of the seed as the Word, we should probably read them as referring not to the seed but to either the situation into which it was sown (as in the case of those along the path) or to the plants that grew from it (as in the cases of the rest).

Obviously, the several responses listed in the parable and

in its interpretation are meant to represent, in terms of either soil conditions or resultant plants, the various kinds of human behavior that can be offered in response to the proclamation of the kingdom. The Word, of course, takes care of itself, infallibly doing what it should in every case; it is no skin off its nose if only the last response listed produces fruitful results. But it is definitely skin off our noses if we respond in ways analogous to one or another of the first three.

The whole purpose of the coming of the Word into the world is to produce people in whom the power of the kingdom will bear fruit. But since the kingdom is fully, albeit mysteriously, present in the Word (since, in other words, the Word's fruitfulness is not in question but is already an accomplished fact), it is chiefly for our sakes that the parable enjoins the necessity of response. The biggest difference made by responses to the Word is the difference they make to us, for us, and in us. They decide not whether the Word will achieve his purposes but whether we will enjoy his achievement — or find ourselves in opposition to it.

Admittedly, I am leaning once again in the direction of a descriptive rather than a prescriptive interpretation of Jesus' words. What he is saying in this parable seems to me to be of a piece with all his other loving, if often sad, commentaries on our condition. He is not threatening some kind of retaliation by the Word against people who fail to make the best response; rather, he is almost wistfully portraying what we miss when we fall short and fail to bear fruit.

And there is the word. In the case of even the most promising of the deficient responses to the sowing of the Word (namely, in the verse about the seed that fell among thorns — Matt. 13:22; Mark 4:18), the result specified is that it becomes *ákarpos,* without fruit, unfruitful. For a plant, the failure to bear fruit is not a punishment visited on it by the seed, but an unhappy declination on the plant's part from what the seed had in mind for it. It is a missing of its own fullness, its own maturity — even, in some deep sense, of its own life. So too with us. If we make deficient responses to the Word, we do not simply get ourselves in dutch; rather, we fail to become ourselves at all.

A look at the word *karpós* (fruit) as Jesus and the New Testament writers use it provides insight. The concordance citations are too numerous to list here, but two in particular stand out. The first is the discourse in which Jesus calls himself the true vine and characterizes his disciples as branches (John 15). The point he makes is complementary to the parable of the Sower: as the branch is not able to bear fruit unless it remains in the vine, so they cannot bear fruit unless they remain in him. In other words, the response most needed is that of simply abiding in the power of the Word himself — which means, in terms of the Sower, neither putting obstacles in the way of the seed nor involving ourselves in the search for other, more plausible responses to it.

The other passage that reinforces the lesson about response in the parable of the Sower is the famous one of Galatians 5:16-26 in which Paul distinguishes between the works of the flesh and the fruits of the Spirit. The *works* are a list of disastrous character traits that the apostle says result from our trying to achieve the fullness of life in our own way: that is, *according to the flesh* (not just the body, please note, but the entire range of human responses — be they physical, mental, or even spiritual — that proceed from our inveterately right-handed wrongheadedness). They are a grim shelf-ful of products, hazardous not only to our health but also to our education and welfare: among other things, they include fornication, witchcraft, strife, envy, and murder.

The *fruits* of the Spirit, however — those results that are not manufactured by our plausible and deliberate efforts but simply allowed to grow unimpeded under the guidance of the Spirit who takes what is the Word's and shows it to us — are, every one of them, truly human traits: love, joy, peace, longsuffering, gentleness, goodness, faith, meekness, temperance. They are not results of, or rewards for, our frantic efforts to make ourselves right; rather, they are the very rightness for which our nature was made, bestowed upon us as a free gift.

It is in the light of such passages as these that the parable of the Sower needs to be seen. It does indeed call for a response from us; but that response is to be one that is appropriate not to the accomplishing of a *work* but to the bearing of *fruit*. The goal it sets for us is not the amassing of deeds, good or bad, but simply the unimpeded experiencing of our own life as the Word abundantly bestows it upon us. And that, as I said, is entirely fitting; because the parable is told to us by none other than the Word himself, whose final concern is nothing less than the reconciled you and me that he longs to offer his heavenly Father. He did not become flesh to display his own virtuosity; he did so to bring us home to his Father's house and sit us down as his bride at the supper of the Lamb. He wills us whole and happy, you see; and the parable of the Sower says he will unfailingly have us so, if only we don't get in the way.

CHAPTER SEVEN

The Lamp and the Growing Seed

Before proceeding to the rest of the parables of the kingdom, I think it is important to take note of the peculiar discontinuity with which they are presented in the Gospels. The writers, instead of running through them one after another, interrupt the natural sequence of these parables in a way that seems illogical — and with a frequency that is surprising.

For one thing, Jesus' interpretations of both the Sower and the Weeds are not given, as we might expect, right at the end of the original parables. Rather, they come only after other material has intervened. I shall have more to say about this when we look at the Weeds (which is separated from its explanation not by an answer to a lone question but by two additional parables plus a reiteration of the observation that Jesus said nothing without a parable). All I want to say here is that my own preferred way of dealing with these insertions is to take them quite seriously — to assume that either Jesus or the Gospel writers felt they were necessary to the argument these parables make for the kingdom and to try to fathom just what that necessity was.

But there is another and even more pervasive pattern of

interruption. Short comments on Jesus' use of the parabolic method, or on its effects, are thrust into the accounts remarkably often. In Matthew, they are inserted at 13:10-17 (between the Sower and its interpretation); at 13:34-35 (just before the interpretation of the Weeds); and at 13:51-52 (where Jesus asks the disciples if they have understood him).

In Mark, the interruptions are at 4:10-12 (parallel to Matt. 13:10-17); and at 4:21-25 (right after the interpretation of the Sower and before the Growing Seed and the Mustard Seed). In Luke, we find them at 8:9-10 (again, parallel to Matt. 13:10-17); at 8:16-18 (parallel to Mark 4:21-25); and at 8:19-21 (where Jesus' relatives are unable to reach him on account of the crowd).

Once again, my disposition is to try to make something of these insertions rather than simply shrug them off as evidence of a not too successful scissors-and-paste job. In any case, the germane passage here is Jesus' parabolic remark about not putting a lamp under a bushel or a bed but on a lampstand — Mark 4:21-22, Luke 8:16-17, and the parallels in Matthew 5:15 and 10:26 — and it seems to me to repay that kind of serious attention. Coming as it does immediately after his explanation of the Sower, I feel it is best expounded by tying it as closely as possible to the notes of catholicity, mystery, actuality, and so on, that he has already begun to attribute to the kingdom.

What do I come up with, then, on the subject of the Lamp? I find that it refers quite nicely to the difficult, scarcely obvious exposition of the parable of the Sower he has just given. The Lamp is the Good News of the sowing of the Word who is the all-sufficient cause of the kingdom; but unless that lamp is set squarely on the lampstand of a relentlessly paradoxical interpretation of the kingdom, its light simply will not be seen. All the easier, more plausible interpretations — those that try to expound the kingdom as parochial, or nonmysterious, or merely virtual — are just so many bushel baskets or beds that can only hide the Lamp's light. And if I add to that my habitual ringing in of John whenever possible, an even fuller meaning of the passage becomes clear: Jesus himself is the Lamp. The incarnate Word — the Light that, coming into the world, lightens every human being — cannot be recognized as the Light he is except on the lampstand of a properly paradoxical, left-handed interpretation of his person and work. Stand him on anything else, and you see not just one more dim bulb like the rest of us; you see no saving Light at all.

Finally, though — as if to reassure us that the paradox by which the hard, almost hidden interpretation is worth the patience it takes to grasp it — he rounds out this particular interruption of himself with an insistence that his apparent hiding of the truth in parables is not an end but a means. "Nothing is hid," he says, "except in order to be made manifest; nor is anything made secret but that it might become plain" (Mark 4:22). The kingdom, like the sown Word, is in the works, and it will settle for nothing less than full manifestation. We are not waiting for its power to come; we believe that it is already here — and that it will inevitably have its perfect and utterly triumphant work.

Fascinatingly enough, this last note convinces me of something else: Jesus' interruptions of himself, far from being mere insertions of stray material, turn out in fact to be artfully constructed bridges to the next development. For as his remarks about the Lamp appear in Mark, they not only wrap up the material on the Sower; they also form the prologue to the first of the explicit parables of the kingdom, namely, the parable of the Growing Seed. Without missing even a beat, Jesus proceeds to give a stunning illustration of the very points he has just been developing.

Consider the Growing Seed. The parable appears only in Mark (4:26-29); and while it once again uses the images of seed and sowing, it contains some remarkable differences from the Sower. First and foremost, it ties the imagery expressly, within the parable itself, to the kingdom: "The kingdom of God," Jesus says, "is as if a man should cast seed upon the ground." Note the strength, even the extravagance, of the comparison: the kingdom is presented as the very thing sown. The kingdom is not the result of the sowing of something quite different from itself (in which it would be contained only virtually, as a plant is contained in a seed); rather, the kingdom as such is present, in all its power, right from the start. Moreover, by the very force of the imagery of sowing, the seed is clearly to be understood as having been sown *in this world,* squarely in the midst of every human and even every earthly condition. This emphasis on the kingdom as a worldly, not just an otherworldly piece of business was already clear in the Sower; but Jesus' repetition of it here as well as later makes me want to underscore it.

Christians have often been lamentably slow to grasp the profound secularity of the kingdom as it is proclaimed in the Gospels. Because Matthew (though not Mark or Luke) uses the phrase "the kingdom of *heaven*" — and perhaps because the greatest number of parables of the kingdom do indeed occur in Matthew — we have frequently succumbed to the temptation to place unwarranted importance on the word "heaven." In any case, we have too often given in to the temptation to picture the kingdom of heaven as if it were something that belonged more properly elsewhere than here. Worse yet, we have conceived of that elsewhere almost entirely in "heavenly" rather than in earthly terms. And all of that, mind you, directly in the face of Scripture's insistences to the contrary.

In the Old Testament, for example, the principal difference between the gods of the heathen and the God who, as
Yahweh, manifested himself to Israel was that, while the
pagan gods occupied themselves chiefly "up there" in the
"council of the gods," Yahweh showed his power principally
"down here" on the stage of history. The pagan deities may
have had their several fiefdoms on earth — pint-size plots
of tribal real estate, outside which they had no interest or
dominion, and even inside which they behaved mostly like
absentee landlords; but their real turf was in the sky, not on
earth. Yahweh, however, claimed two distinctions. Even on
their heavenly turf, he insisted, it was he and not they who
were in charge. And when he came down to earth, he acted
as if the whole place was his own back yard. In fact, it was
precisely by his overcoming them on utterly earthly ground,
in and through his chosen people, that he claimed to have
beaten them even on their heavenly home court. What he
did on earth was done in heaven, and vice versa, because
he alone, as the One Yahweh, was the sole proprietor of
both.

In the New Testament, that inseparability of heavenly
concerns from earthly ones is, if anything, even more strenu-
ously maintained. The kingdom Jesus proclaims is *at hand,
planted here, at work in this world.* The Word sown is none
other than *God himself incarnate.* By his death and resurrection at Jerusalem in A.D. 29, he reconciles everything, everywhere, to himself — whether they be things on earth or
things in heaven. And at the end, when he makes all things
new, he makes not just a new heaven but a new earth — a
glorified re-creation of nothing less than his old stamping
ground. The Bible's last chapters proclaim a heaven and
earth more inextricably intertwined than ever. Whatever else
the "New Jerusalem" may signify, it says plainly that the
final "heaven" will be as earthy as the eschatological earth

will be heavenly — and that that's the way it is going to be forever.

Indeed, it is worth noting that most uses of the words "heaven" or "heavenly" in the New Testament bear little relation to the meanings we have so unscripturally attached to them. For us, heaven is an unearthly, humanly irrelevant condition in which bed-sheeted, paper-winged spirits sit on clouds and play tinkly music until their pipe-cleaner halos drop off from boredom. As we envision it, it contains not one baby's bottom, not one woman's breast, not even one man's bare chest — much less a risen basketball game between glorified "shirts" and "skins." But in Scripture, it is a city with boys and girls playing in the streets; it is buildings put up by a Department of Public Works that uses amethysts for cinder blocks and pearls as big as the Ritz for gates; and indoors, it is a dinner party to end all dinner parties at the marriage supper of the Lamb. It is, in short, earth wedded, not earth jilted. It is the world as the irremovable apple of God's eye.

And that (to come to the end of a not unearthly digression) is what Jesus is proclaiming in the parable of the Growing Seed. The kingdom itself, he insists, is the very thing that is sown. And in the rest of the parable, he drives home, with a clarity matched almost nowhere else, the absolute sovereignty of that kingdom over the earth it wills to make its home. There are no references at all here to the dangers that hostility might pose for it; nor are there even any references to the detrimental or beneficial effects of the various responses that human beings might make to it. Instead, Jesus ignores these matters entirely. As Jesus depicts it, once the man in the parable has sown the seed, he does nothing more than mind his own and not the seed's business. He goes to bed at night and gets up in the morning — and then he shops at the supermarket, unclogs the sink, whips up a gourmet supper, plays chamber music with his friends, watches the eleven o'clock news, and goes to bed again. And he does that and nothing but that, day after day after day — while all along, the seed that is the kingdom sprouts and grows in a way that he himself simply *knows nothing about.*

But then comes one of the most startling statements in all of Scripture: *Automátē hē gē karpophoreí,* Jesus says; the earth (and all of it, mind you: good, bad, or indifferent) bears fruit *of itself,* automatically. Just put the kingdom into the world, he says in effect; put it into any kind of world — not only into a world of hotshot responders or spiritual pros, but into a world of sinners, deadbeats, and assorted other poor excuses for humanity (which, interestingly enough, is the only world available anyway) — and it will come up a perfect kingdom all by itself: "first the blade, then the ear, then the full grain in the ear." It takes its time about it, to be sure; but the time it takes is entirely its own, not anyone else's. There is not a breath about crop failure, any more than there is about the depredations of the devil or the knuckleheadedness of humanity. There is only the proclamation of a catholic sowing that, mysteriously but effectively, results in a catholic growth toward a catholic harvest.

At this point, though, I detect in your mind a premature readiness to utter a sigh of relief: "Finally!" you think. "The harvest! And about time! Enough of this dangerously indiscriminate catholicity. Too much of this silence about all the criminal types who will obviously take this omnium-gatherum gospel as permission to go right on committing their felonies, even in the New Jerusalem. At last, Jesus is about to threaten the world with the eschatological come-uppance we know and love so well."

In this parable, however, your mind's desire is doomed

to disappointment. To be sure, there are other passages (notably the parable of the Weeds) where Jesus does indeed use the word *therismós,* "harvest," to introduce the notion of millennial police work. But not here. Here he simply contents himself with a last line not one bit more discriminating than the rest of the parable: "But when the fruit is ripe, at once he puts in the sickle, because the harvest has come." Not a word, you see, about separating the wheat from the weeds. Not a syllable about getting the baddies out of the kingdom and burning them up in fire unquenchable. Why?

You could argue, of course, that the omission is a space- and time-saving one — that because Jesus supplies those details elsewhere, they should simply be understood as applying here too. But I don't like that. Jesus, it seems to me, achieved his status as a world-class teacher not only by what he put into his utterances but by what he left out of them as well. Whenever he felt himself in the presence of minds that were itching to jump to their favorite conclusions about how God should run the universe, he deliberately refused to give them a platform to jump from. As I tried to show earlier, he did that in the parable of the Sower when he paradoxically raised the Jew-Gentile question by not raising it at all, thus depriving his hearers of the assurances they felt a proper Messiah should give. And he does it even more clearly in John 6 where the whole dialogue between him and the Judean Jews is one long exercise in messianic foot-dragging — with Jesus insisting right to the end on giving them naught for their comfort.

And that, it strikes me, is just what he is doing here. Every last man Jack (or Jill) of us — and every bit as much back then as right now — is an eschatology junkie. We are so consumed with the idea that wrongs must be set right and that evildoers must be run out of the New Jerusalem on a chiliastic rail that we convince ourselves the Holy City can actually be brought into being by means of cops-and-robbers games. Our favorite solutions to the world's deep and humanly intractable problems with sin are punching people in the nose, locking them up in the slammer, and — failing all else — buying them a one-way ride out of town in the electric chair. Worse yet, when we come to the point (as we always do) of giving God advice about how to deal eternally with the same problems, we simply concoct eternal variations of the same procedures.

I am aware, of course, that Scripture quite plainly speaks of just those sorts of activities on the part of God. And even though you might not expect me to say so after that last tirade, I am perfectly willing to take such right-handed strong-arm stuff seriously: that is, as just as inspired as — but not, please note, as more inspired than — the Bible's other, more left-handed ways of talking about the ultimate triumph of divine justice. But. But, but, but: *that is not what we are talking about here.* And for even more of a *but:* that is the very subject that Jesus is scrupulously avoiding at the end of the parable of the Growing Seed. His subject is the utterly fundamental one of *how* the kingdom grows, of *the means by which* the city is built. It is not the relatively minor one of how the Divine Police Department keeps muggers off the streets of the New Jerusalem.

The kingdom grows, he says, because the kingdom is already planted. It grows of itself and in its own good time. Above all, it grows *we know not how.* Any bright ideas we might have about the subject will always and everywhere be the wrong ideas. Indeed, their wrongness will be proved simply by our having them; because if the kingdom could have been made to grow in this world by bright ideas, it would have sprouted up all over the place six times a day ever since Adam. But it never did and it never will, except in a mystery that remains resolutely beyond our moralizing, score-evening comprehension.

In my view, it is for just that reason that the Growing Seed has nothing in it about God's ultimate cleanup operation. Jesus withholds from his hearers at this point anything that might distract them from the saving mystery and bog them down once again in hopeless plausibilities. Admittedly, in the next group of kingdom passages (the Weeds, the Mustard Seed, the Leaven, the comment about Jesus' saying nothing without a parable, and the interpretation of the Weeds), he does indeed give his hearers grist for their eschatological morality mills. But — and I think this will be borne out as we proceed — he does it with at least some reluctance. In Mark and Luke, of course, he does it not at all at this juncture. On balance, therefore, the synoptics make out a fair case for looking a lot longer and harder at the constitution of the kingdom before we engross ourselves in its prison statistics.

CHAPTER EIGHT

The Weeds

Perhaps the best way to deal with the portion of the Gospel that runs from Jesus' parable of the Weeds through his eventual interpretation of it (Matt. 13:24-43) is simply to proceed through the material in order, noting as we go both the points that corroborate the general approach I have been taking and those that call it into question.

Jesus' first version of the parable of the Weeds, like his first version of the Sower, is a straight story about farming: he resists yet again the temptation to say what it means until after he has unburdened himself of other, and seemingly unconnected remarks. Farmers and gardeners, of course, may raise an eyebrow at the story's strictly agricultural aspects. The practice of not pulling out weeds until harvest time is no way to run a farm. All that such neglect insures is two undesirable results. First, it contributes to the choking out of the good plants that Jesus deplored in the Sower; second, it guarantees a bumper crop of unwanted weed seeds to plague the next season's planting. Nevertheless, the parable as told simply flouts these truths of agronomy in order to make its theological point. Maybe Jesus was just not as good a gardener as he was a carpenter (his comments about building houses on proper foundations [Matt. 7:24-27] sound a lot more like the words of an expert). In any case, his real trade was Messiah-ing, about which, fittingly enough, he wrote the book. Back, then, to the way he actually begins the parable of the Weeds.

"Another parable he put before them," the Gospel says (Matthew, as if to underscore the cohesiveness of the whole string of kingdom parables, starts three of them with the word *állē,* "another," and two more with *pálin,* "again"); "the kingdom of heaven may be likened to a man sowing good seed in his field."

At first blush, Jesus seems to be shifting away here from his insistence (for instance, in the Growing Seed) that the kingdom as such is what is sown. Even more, he seems to be setting up the story in such a way that, when he does come to interpret it, he will be forced to represent himself not as the Word or the seed sown but simply as the one who does the sowing. However, the phrase he uses here for "good seed" is a bit of a departure from the references he has so far made to the subject. In the Greek, it is *kalón spérma,* and a brief look at the concordance turns up some fascinating information.

In the New Testament, there are some forty occurrences of the word *spérma.* In the old days, it was common practice to English all of them with the word "seed"; but *spérma* only rarely refers to the actual thing planted. Indeed, by my reckoning, there are only four such airtight references: two in the first telling of the parable of the Weeds (Matt. 13:24 and 27) and two in the immediately following parable of the Mustard Seed (Matt. 13:32 and Mark 4:31) where Jesus says that when the seed is sown, it is *mikróteron . . . pánton tōn spermátēn,* "smaller than all the seeds." By contrast, in most of its occurrences (over thirty of them), it is used to refer not strictly to seed as seed but to *the progeny that comes from* seed. *Spérma Ábraham,* "seed of Abraham," is the commonest citation; it refers obviously not to Abraham's sperm cells but to his descendants — that is, to what grows from the seed rather than to the seed itself.

It seems to me that it is ultimately this force that the word *spérma* takes on in the parable of the Weeds — and for that matter, in the remaining handful of places where it does not refer to the descendants of human beings. True enough, when Jesus initially tells the parable in its unexplained form, *planted seed* is the fairest interpretation of the word; but just as plainly, when he comes to identify the "good seed" in his allegorization of the parable (Matt. 13:38), he makes it refer more to what has grown up as a result than to what was planted to begin with. "The good seed," he says, "are the *sons of the kingdom,*" that is, the offspring of the kingdom, those whose lives are the flowering and fructifying of what was sown by the Son of Man. Interestingly, too, it is just this usage of "good seed" (and "bad seed") that eventually made its way into English: "he's bad seed," for example, refers not simply to a man's origin but to his subsequent character and actions.

At any rate, whatever sense we assign to *spérma* at this point, there is no question about the force of the word "sow": Jesus is referring to the broadcast planting of an entire field. Once again, he presents the action of his parable in a way that necessitates a sounding of the note of catholicity in its interpretation. By speaking only of one man's field, and by avoiding any hint of a partial sowing of that field, he clearly indicates that there are no places — and by extension, no times and no people — in which the kingdom is not already at work.

But then Jesus continues with a whole string of fascinating details: "While everyone was sleeping," he says, "the man's enemy came and sowed *zizánia,* weeds, among the wheat and went away." Note first the "sleeping." What is referred to is not culpable napping on the job but, as in the Growing Seed, the normal nocturnal habits of even the most dedicated farmers. They have no duties to the sown crop that need to be done at night; every positive measure called for has already been done by day. Other things being equal, the seed in the ground will do the rest of the job entirely on its own. The mystery, in other words — the mystery of both the sowing of seed and the sowing of the kingdom — can, will, and does fend nicely for itself, thank you very much. Furthermore, while Jesus develops the imagery of the parable of the Sower in such a way that the mystery itself seems in danger (from the birds, from the rocky ground, from the thorns), the parable of the Weeds gives no hint of such perils. From start to finish, the working of the seed is not seriously threatened at all.

Something does go wrong, of course, but it is important to be clear about how the parable presents it: the man's *enemy* comes and sows weeds. But since the weeds in no way seem to interfere with the growing of the wheat, it is the word "enemy" that should become the crux of the interpretation. It is not danger to the crop's growth but inconvenience to the farmer and his servants that lies at the heart of the agricultural-theological dilemma in the parable. The servants, naturally enough, have the most intense feelings about the inconvenience, and it is they who have the bright idea of taking immediate and direct action against the weeds. The farmer, though, seems to have in mind some grander strategy — one that involves not fighting a minor battle against transitory inconveniences but winning an entire war, once and for all, against his enemy.

In other words, the parable says that *doing nothing* is, for the time being, the preferred response to evil. It insists

that the mysterious, paradoxical tactic of noninterference is
the only one that can be effective in the time frame within
which the servants are working. No matter that they may
have plausible proposals for dealing with the menace as they
see it; their very proposals, the farmer tells them, are more
of a menace than anything else. To be sure, he goes on to
assure them that at some later, riper time, he will indeed
interfere to a fare-thee-well with his enemy's plans. But the
principal thrust of the parable, especially as Jesus first tells
it, is that until the harvest, the "evil" is to be suffered, not
resisted. The parable's main point, in short, is not eschatological redress of wrongs, but *present forbearance of them.*
And even though Jesus' subsequent interpretation of the
story tilts it mightily in the direction of eschatology, his
insistence on nonresistance to the enemy's troublemaking
still comes through clearly enough.

But that is to get ahead of the story. Note next what it
is that Jesus says the enemy sows among the wheat: *zizánia,*
weeds, tares — specifically darnel, *Lolium temulentum,* an
annual grass that, with its long, slender awns, or bristles,
looks very much like wheat indeed. And what does *that* say
about the present relationship between the kingdom and
the evil in the world?

Well, it seems to me to say that programs and, a fortiori,
pogroms designed to get rid of evil are, by the muddle-
headedness of the world and the craft and subtlety of the
enemy, doomed to do exactly what the farmer suggests they
will do. Since the only troops available to fight the battle
are either too confused or too busy to recognize the real
difference between good and evil, all they will accomplish
by their frantic pulling out of the weeds is the tearing up
of the wheat right along with them. Worse yet, since good
and evil in this world commonly inhabit not only the same
field but even the same individual human beings — since,

101

that is, there are no unqualified good guys any more than there are any unqualified bad guys — the only result of a truly dedicated campaign to get rid of evil will be the abolition of literally everybody.

Indeed, that puts the finger on the whole purpose of the enemy's sowing of the weeds. He has no power against goodness in and of itself: the wheat is in the field, the kingdom is in the world, and there is not a thing he can do about any of it. Evil, like darnel, is a counterfeit of reality, not reality itself. It is a parasite on being, not being itself.

As the parable develops its point, though, the enemy turns out not to need anything more than negative power. He has to act only minimally on his own to wreak havoc in the world; mostly, he depends on the forces of goodness, *insofar as he can sucker them into taking up arms against the confusion he has introduced,* to do his work. That is precisely why the enemy *goes away* after sowing the weeds: he has no need whatsoever to hang around. Unable to take positive action anyway — having no real power to muck up the operation — he simply sprinkles around a generous helping of darkness and waits for the children of light to get flustered enough to do the job for him. Goodness itself, in other words, if it is sufficiently committed to plausible, right-handed, strong-arm methods, will in the very name of goodness do all and more than all that evil ever had in mind.

One word in passing. If you are worrying that this exposition might form the basis of a case for pacifism, you should continue to worry. But you should also make a distinction. The parable, it seems to me, does not say that resistance to evil is morally wrong, only that it is salvifically ineffective. You may, therefore, make out as many cases as you like for just wars, capital punishment, or any other sensible, right-handed solution to the presence of malefactors on earth; but you must not assume that such solutions will necessarily make the world a better place. You may, in short, take the sword, but you should also remember that those who do so inevitably perish by the sword — descriptively, not prescriptively. God does not punish people for being nonpacifists; war alone is punishment enough. But even though pacifism seems not to be enjoined by Scripture, we should note for the record that the parable of the Weeds suggests that — *pro tem* at least — God himself is a pacifist. You don't have to be one, therefore; but *pro* the only *tem* you have, you might find the company quite good.

Back to the parable. "So when the plants came up and bore fruit [*karpón*]," Jesus continues, "then the weeds also appeared." The mystery of goodness is going swimmingly: the kingdom is coming along *automátē,* quite of its own accord, and its growth and fructifying are actual, catholic facts. But the mystery of iniquity seems unfortunately to be doing just as well. True to its nature as a counterfeit of reality, it too pretends to catholicity and actuality. The weeds may not be real wheat, but they look just like it; if the servants can be inveigled into taking up arms against them, a truly catholic and actual disaster can be brewed.

And one almost is. Coming to the farmer, the servants are totally preoccupied with the problem of evil. "You sowed good seed in your field, didn't you, Sir?" they ask him. "Where then did the weeds come from?" Just like two thousand years' worth of Christian theologians — though more excusably, perhaps, since the workers were ignorant of the crucifixion — their first intellectual efforts are directed, not to finding out how they should act in the presence of evil, but to looking for an explanation of it that they can understand. "If God is good, why is the world bad?" they ask in effect; "why does he allow all these terrible things to happen?"

Fascinating though such a question may be, there is a

distinct note of pointlessness about it. It's not that it is unanswerable; it's just that there are so many contradictory answers to it that they produce only confusion. Consider just three possible replies to the question just raised: (1) God is *not* good; so why should the world be any better? (2) God *is* good, but he is also not very powerful (or smart or caring or whatever), so things are just beyond his competence. (3) God is good — and brilliant, clever, loving, and anything else you would like to mention — but for some reason he also has enemies who make a lot of trouble.

Pause here for a moment and note two things. First, not a single one of these answers — nor any other answer that could imaginably be given — is the least help to you when it comes to actually dealing with evil. All that any of them addresses is the distinctly armchair problem your intellectual bookkeeping department is having with a divine operation over which it has no control. The only possible action that can come out of your concern is the bestowal or withholding of your personal approbation — something that, in either case, makes no difference whatsoever. If a mugger is stabbing you with impunity, your biggest problem is hardly whether you can manage to approve or disapprove of a cosmic Somebody who, by design or default, makes such unpleasant behavior possible.

Second, note that all the answers to theological posers about God and evil serve only to raise more questions. Particularly the third answer listed above, which is, obviously, the one closest to the reply the farmer gave his servants. "Disgraceful!" the indignant question-maven snorts when he learns that God, like the farmer, has enemies. "What kind of God would put up with such nonsense? Why doesn't he just swat them? Do you mean to tell me he's not powerful enough? Do you expect me to believe in a Supreme Being like that?"

But enough. To the credit of the servants in the parable, they do not go down that theological blind alley. Instead of trying to find a way of holding somebody responsible for the enemy's inconveniencing of them, they content themselves with inquiring about possible steps they might take. "Do you want us," they ask the farmer, "to go out and pull up the weeds?" Ultimately, of course, that reaction was not much more germane than an abstract worrying of the bone of theodicy; but at least it displayed a cooperative rather than a contentious spirit — and it should stand as a warning to all theologizers.

The Bible's only real answer to the problem of evil is, like it or not, the same as the farmer's answer to the question posed by the presence of the weeds: *"An enemy hath done this"* (KJV). That may play hob with your notion of God, but it's all the answer you are going to get from Scripture. And after it, there are only two other important questions left. The first is, "Whose side are you on?" — a question, please note, that the servants got an "A" on. And the second is, "Whose methods do you propose to use in dealing with the problem?" On that one, alas, they got an "F." But if we can manage to learn from their mistake, we have a good chance of passing the whole test.

"No!" the farmer says to them. "Pull up evil, and you'll pull up goodness right along with it." But then comes the most remarkable word in the whole parable: *"Áphete* [let, permit, suffer] both to grow together until the harvest." Simply to pause over this statement, however, is not enough; it calls for a full-scale application of the brakes — a complete parking of the theological car in order to take in an incredibly rich landscape.

The verb *aphíēmi* (infinitive: *aphiénai* or *aphíein*), from which *áphete* is conjugated, has two major meanings in the New Testament. The first is the one represented by its use in this parable: send away, let go, leave, permit — not to mention about ten other similar senses that flow quite directly from the formulation of the word: *apó (aph')* is a prepositional prefix meaning "from"; and *híēmi* is a verb meaning "send, let go, dismiss." As translated into Latin, *aphiénai* came out as, among other things, *dimittere, omittere, emittere, admittere, permittere,* and *remittere;* and due to the influence of Latin upon English, almost all of those senses — expressed by either Anglo-Saxon or Latin roots — were simply imported into the English versions of the Scriptures.

But the second meaning of the word is the fascinating one here: *aphiénai,* when applied (via the Latin *dimittere* or *remittere*) to debts, trespasses, sins, and so on, comes out in English as "forgive." A glance at a concordance shows how important this use is: in the King James Version, for example, forty-seven of the hundred-fifty-six occurrences of *aphiénai* are translated by "forgive" (the rest are Englished in various ways — with "leave," in fifty-two places, as the commonest rendering).

Time out for a commercial on the concordance as the best of all possible aids to Bible study. If we take seriously our belief that the Holy Spirit presided over the entire process by which the Bible was formed, then clearly there can be no better commentary on Scripture than Scripture itself. And a concordance is the preeminent device by which that biblical self-commentary can be grasped — especially if the concordance is so arranged as to allow the readers (whether they know Greek or not) to search out all the occurrences of a word not only in English but in the original Greek.

This is crucial because, after all, it was upon authors writing in Greek — and upon a Christian community responding to their work in Greek — that the Spirit sent the guidance of his inspiration. Consider the present case of the *áphete* in the parable of the Weeds. A modern reader with access to nothing but English would see it translated as "Let both grow . . ." and simply read on. But when that *áphete* was read in the early Christian church — say, during the liturgy on the Lord's day — it would have rung a very large bell in the congregation's mind. They had just prayed (or shortly would pray) the Lord's prayer: *"Áphes,"* they would have said, *"Forgive* us our debts, as we also *aphíemen,* forgive, our debtors." On hearing, therefore, that the farmer's answer to the malice of the enemy was yet another *áphete,* they might well have grasped the Holy Spirit's exalted pun immediately: the malice, the evil, the badness that is manifest in the real world and in the lives of real people is not to be dealt with by attacking or abolishing the things or persons in whom it dwells; rather, it is to be dealt with only by an *áphesis,* by a *letting be* that was a *forgiveness,* that was a *suffering* — that was even a *permission* — all rolled into one.

Notice I said only that they *might* have grasped that. A good many Christian theologians, even among those who know Greek, have managed to miss the point completely. Indeed, the first objection usually raised to letting evil be — let alone to forgiving it — takes the form of agitated moralistic hand-wringing: "But if you simply tell people in advance that they're going to be forgiven, won't they just go straight out and take that as *permission* to sin? Don't we have to keep them scared out of their wits by continually harping on the big difference between forgiveness and permission?"

I have a number of replies to all that. The first is, *"What* big difference? In Greek, the same word is used for both." The second is, "There's no difference between them at all. If you're an utterly serious forgiver, and if you make your forgiving disposition known to a solid brass snake-in-the-grass, he will obviously play you for the sucker you are as often as he feels like it: what do you think the world, the flesh, and the devil thought about a Jesus who died on the cross instead of nuking his enemies?" The third is, "What on earth are you talking about? God, in the act of creating you, gave you permission to do any damned fool thing you could manage to bring off. Forgiveness neither increases nor decreases the level of God's permissiveness; instead, it just fishes us out of the otherwise inescapable quicksand we so stupidly got ourselves into and says, 'There! Isn't that better?'" My fourth and final reply, though, is, "Of course there's a difference; and it's a whopping one. But since even that makes no difference at all to either the farmer in the parable or to Jesus on the cross — or, for that matter, to any Christian committed to forgiving his skunk of a brother seventy times seven times — why harp on it?"

Follow that up. On the basis of the parable as told, the farmer has announced, publicly and in advance (do you seriously think the servants told nobody about his crazy plan to leave the weeds alone?), that his enemy is quite free to come back any night he chooses and sow any weeds he likes. Not just more *zizánia*, but purslane, dock, bindweed, pigweed, or even — when he finally runs out of seriously mischievous ideas — New Zealand spinach.

There is more. On the basis of Jesus' ministry as lived and died, God has announced the very same thing. No enemy — not the devil, not you, not me, and not anybody else — is going to get it in the neck, in this life, for any evil he has done. The Old Testament to the contrary notwithstanding — and despite all the subsequent tub-thumping by "God is not mocked" Christians who seem unaware that a New Testament was given because there was no way in which the Old one could break the entail of sin — Jesus on the cross doesn't threaten his enemies, he forgives them: *"áphes,"* he says, one last time.

And then there's the clincher. On the basis of Jesus' ministry as risen, there is no change in that policy. He comes forth from the tomb and ascends into heaven with nail prints in his hands and feet and a spear wound in his risen side — with eternal, glorious scars to remind God, angels, and us that he is not about to go back on his word from the cross.

Oh, of course. I know that by now you are mighty tired of all this emphasis on the Divine Sweetness. You are just itching to remind me that at the harvest, the weeds are going to be bound up in bundles and burned in an appropriately eschatological fire. And so they are. And to finish off the text, so is the wheat going to be gathered into the barn. But if I may try your patience just one minute more, let me ask you to consider the *proportions* of this parable as Jesus first tells it. The words that you have all along been holding your breath to hear constitute only two thirds of its final verse. The rest of the parable — Matthew 13:24-30a — is entirely about the *áphesis* of evil, not about the avenging of it.

To be sure, Jesus does indeed end on the note of the ultimate triumph of justice. Why? Well, presumably because it stresses a truth: God is in charge, and he will, under eschatological circumstances, get his own way. But the great bulk of the parable is told to stress another, and equally central truth: namely, that in the present circumstances of the world (the only circumstances, please note, in which we now find ourselves), the *mystery of the kingdom* is likewise quite in charge and thoroughly capable of getting its own way. It is sown, sprouted, and bearing fruit: all the *zizánia* in the world haven't got a finger they can effectually lift against it.

But I think there is also another reason why Jesus gives the ultimate vindication such short shrift at this point. As I said, the human race is hooked on eschatology: give us one drag on it, and we proceed to party away our whole forgiven life in fantasies about a final score-settling session that none of us, except for forgiveness, could possibly survive. Jesus, it seems to me, senses that about us as he reaches the end of this parable. "Well," he thinks to himself, "I gave them the fire and brimstone stuff they were dying to hear; and I'm glad, I guess, because after all, it *is* the truth. But oh, how I hate to think of what they're going to do with it: throw them just one eschatological dog biscuit like that, and they'll never stop yapping. Let me see. What to tell them next? H'm. Probably I should get off the end-of-the-world business completely. One thing's for sure though: I'm definitely not going to say another word about these damned weeds until I'm good and ready."

CHAPTER NINE

The Mustard Seed and the Leaven

Before we proceed, let me give a roundup of the box scores that the parable of the Weeds has so far chalked up under the five headings I have been using for the parables of the kingdom.

On *catholicity* it gets high marks. Not only does it portray the kingdom as having been sown everywhere in the world but, for the first time, it introduces into the narrative a parallel insistence on what we might call the catholicity of evil. Indeed, it is just this grappling with the radical intermixture of goodness and badness in the world — with the "problem of evil" the parable so succinctly raises — that sets it off as a remarkable step forward in Jesus' teaching about the kingdom.

The note of *mystery* is likewise expanded to apply to evil as well as good: both the weeds and the wheat grow from hidden beginnings as seed. But the most notable heightening of the element of mystery lies in Jesus' attempt, again for the first time, to assign a reason for the presence of evil. By attributing it to an enemy who works surreptitiously, at night, he makes the mystery of evil yet another parallel to the mystery of the kingdom. It is a counterfeit, of course;

111

but precisely because of that, hasty and overenthusiastic attempts to get it out of circulation are flatly discouraged.

As far as the *actual, present working* of the kingdom is concerned, the parable of the Weeds scores just as well as any so far. In fact, there is even less room left for virtualism in its interpretation than there was, say, in the Sower. The wheat, from start to finish, successfully does its proper work. The enemy may be a gigantic nuisance; but he is never a serious, ultimate threat.

But it is under the headings of *hostility* and *response* that the parable of the Weeds tops all previous scores. As I pointed out in connection with *mystery*, the enemy's machinations are presented in images that are supremely suitable to the father of lies. There is no openness here, none of the simplicity that characterizes the straightforward hostility of the birds or the rocky ground or the thorns. Rather, there is the full-blown paradox of the appearance of evil in a situation where there is absolutely no reason to expect it ("You sowed *good* seed, didn't you? How come, then . . . ?"). Finally, though, in its development of the note of response to the kingdom, the parable of the Weeds really breaks the record.

When we think of the subject of response, especially with regard to sacred subjects, our inveterate Pelagianism — our tendency to think that our own moral efforts are necessary to the plan of salvation — leads us to set up scenarios in which the work of the kingdom simply will not go forward without our cooperation. And that in turn — since we are much better at antagonistic responses than at positive ones — leads us to imagine that the best way for us to give the kingdom a helping hand is to take up arms as promptly as possible against the enemies of the Lord. But the parable of the Weeds stands in direct contrast to any such moral muscle-flexing.

Only God, it says, only the Farmer in charge of the

universal operation, knows how to deal successfully with evil. And note well that his sole competence applies both here and hereafter — both now, during the growing season, and then, at the harvest. Here and now, while the mystery of evil is intermingled with the mystery of the kingdom, he wills to deal with it only by *áphesis:* by forgiveness, by permission, by letting it be. But there and then, in the eschatological fullness of the kingdom — as that fullness is portrayed in the rest of the New Testament — he still deals with it in terms of something that is a mystery to us now, namely, the mystery of the Resurrection.

When we dwell too simplistically on the Final Judgment, we almost always picture it as the day when God finally takes off the gloves of mystery with which he has so far handled the world and gives his enemies a decisive taste of eschatological bare knuckles. That image, however, leaves one important truth out of account: the judgment occurs only *after* the general resurrection of the dead. And since the resurrection of the dead (of the just and the unjust alike) is something that happens to them solely by virtue of Jesus' resurrection — about which we have very little unparadoxical information — we should be very slow to imagine scenarios for it that are based on simplistic extrapolations of our present experience. Everything that happens after the second coming of Jesus — judgment, heaven, and even hell — happens within the triumphantly reconciling power of his death and resurrection. We simply don't know how or to what degree that power affects the eschatological situation.

Take, for example, the question of whether *we* are in a position to discuss the meaning or even the possibility of ultimate human rejection of the reconciliation. To be sure, Scripture says clearly enough that the sovereign, healing power of Jesus can and will be refused by some. I have no

113

problem with that. What I do object to, however, are the hell-enthusiasts who act as if God's whole New Testament method of dealing with evil will, in the last day, simply go back to some Old Testament "square one" — as if Jesus hadn't done a blessed or merciful thing in between, and as if we could, therefore, skip all the paradoxes of mercy when we talk about the Last Day and simply concentrate on plain old gun-barrel justice.

Admittedly, the Bible talks about all sorts of creatures going to hell. But my point is that if they do go, they go even there in the power of a resurrection by which God in Christ has reconciled all things to himself, hell included. There is no one anywhere in the final scheme of things who is floating around in his own old unrisen state. Resurrection is not a reward for the chosen few; it is the only game there is in the whole eschatological town. And that resurrection, I submit, while it will presumably not be a mystery to anybody, good or bad, *then,* remains very much of a mystery to us *now.* We don't know beans about what the actual, ultimate dynamics of people's situations will be in that day; so we should be a bit more reluctant than we are to rattle on so blithely about it in our own day — especially in ways that practically ignore the mystery that governs all days, first, middle, or last.

In any case, even Jesus himself seems to exhibit a touch of just that reluctance. Having broached the problem of evil to his hearers — and having waved under their noses the tempting bone of millennial grievance-settling — he suddenly drops both subjects completely. In my view, he does so because he senses that his hearers are doing a lot of premillennial salivating over postmillennial justice. And because he judges that sort of thing hazardous to their grip not only on the mystery of the kingdom but especially on the mystery of the divine *áphesis* of evil, he simply puts off giving it to them. If you don't like that view, however, feel free to sit loose to it: nobody really knows what Jesus *thought* anyway. The important thing is what he *said* next, namely, the parables of the Mustard Seed and of the Leaven.

All three of the synoptic Gospels contain the Mustard Seed (see the chart in chapter 5), so a look at the similarities and differences of the accounts suggests itself as a way of approaching it. Matthew, as I have noted, stresses continuity by beginning with the words "another [*állēn*] parable," and he sets forth the parable itself with his by now usual introduction: "The kingdom of heaven is like. . . ." But Mark and Luke begin by having Jesus pose a question. In Mark, Jesus asks, "How shall we compare the kingdom of God, or by what parable shall we set it forth?" In Luke, he eschews the editorial or majestic plural and simply asks, "What is the kingdom of God like, and to what shall I compare it?"

Obviously, it is entirely possible to take these utterances simply as rhetorical questions, mere throat-clearing introductions to the point he is about to make. For all I know, that may even be the best thing to do with them. But they do suggest another line of interpretation — one that takes into account Jesus' sudden shift away from the eschatological problems posed by evil. While the juxtaposition of the Weeds and the Mustard Seed occurs only in Matthew, in both Mark and Luke the Mustard Seed can still be seen as an attempt on Jesus' part to distance himself from eschatology. His beginning with a question, therefore, can be taken simply as his wondering out loud just how to do so. In Mark, the Mustard Seed follows the Growing Seed — which, albeit glancingly, does refer to both *sickle* and *harvest*. In Luke, however, both it and the parable of the Leaven occur in the midst of a welter of eschatological passages. In short, no matter where the Mustard Seed appears, it stands in some contrast to its immediate setting. I do not find it preposterous, therefore, to imagine that it came out the way it did precisely because Jesus — in response to his own question — decided that such contrast was more than called for.

At any rate, what he says the kingdom is like is *kókkō sinápeōs,* a mustard seed. Note once again that the kingdom is the very thing sown, not something that results from the sowing of a seed other than itself. Note, too, some minor differences in the accounts: In Matthew and Luke, it is compared to a seed that a man took and sowed in his field (Luke, for some reason — perhaps because he was a physician with a bit of a *Better Homes and Gardens* approach to agriculture — has the man put the seed into his *garden*). Mark, however, goes straight to the point that Matthew takes his time getting to (and that Luke never gets to at all), namely, that the kingdom is like a mustard seed "which, when it is sown upon the ground, is smaller than all the seeds on the earth." Score another point, therefore, in both the *catholicity* and the *mystery* columns. The *whole* field is sown (Mark uses the word *gē,* meaning both the "ground" and the "earth" — with the pun, I like to think, intended). And it is sown in a way that is hidden: mustard seeds, while by no means the all-time smallness champions that Jesus makes them, are at any rate a lot smaller than peach pits.

But it is on the score of the *actual working* of the kingdom — and in particular, of its successful working — that the parable of the Mustard Seed scores the most points: the seed grows up (to put all three accounts into one basket) into something bigger than all vegetables (Matthew, Mark); it puts forth big branches (Mark); and it becomes a tree, a *déndron* (Matthew, Luke), under whose shade (Mark) the birds of the heaven make their nests (Matthew, Mark, Luke). "Tree," of course, may strike those of us who are gardeners as a touch of excessive vividness, but the comparison still stands: even the common garden mustard plant is taller than brussels sprouts or untrellised cucumbers. And while bird's nests are not what we would expect to find in one, we'd be a lot more surprised to discover them in bush beans. Field corn would be something else, admittedly . . . but it would also be an illustration of pointless exegesis, so skip it.

The real point of the parable is the marvelous discrepancy between the hiddenness of the kingdom at its sowing and the lush, manifest exuberance of it in its final, totally successful fruition. "So you want me to tell you about the end of the story, do you?" Jesus seems to be saying. "Well, here it is; but without a word about evil to throw you into your usual eschatological tailspin. All you get here is the peaceable kingdom: the sun shining in the sky, birds flying in and out of the shade, and all the little ones twittering away forever and ever. No elements of *hostility* to tempt you to think the kingdom won't arrive unless you ride shotgun for it. And no elements of *response* to suggest it might need your cooperation in order to come out right — unless, of course, you consider larking around in the trees a proper response; in which case, *that* I'll let you have."

And then, as if to continue driving home the same point, Jesus segues straight into the parable of the Leaven. I shall not even try to restrain my natural enthusiasm for this parable. Not only does its reference to yeast delight my deepest roots (I have for decades made my own bread, without even once losing my fascination with the process); even more, it corroborates, with what has to be a divine economy of words, everything I have been trying to say. Let me comment on it then — with not the slightest attempt to imitate the divine brevity.

The parable appears in Matthew and Luke; and with the exception of the fact that Luke begins it with a question ("To what shall I liken the kingdom of God," instead of the

Matthean "Another parable he spoke to them"), the two accounts can be dealt with as one. The kingdom, Jesus tells his hearers, is like "leaven [*zýmę̄*], which a woman took and hid [*(en)ékrypsen*] in three measures of flour [*aleúrou sáta tría*], until the whole [*hólon*] was leavened."

Let it simply be noted in passing that the surrogate for God in this parable is a woman. Set that down, along with Jesus' calling himself a mother hen, as evidence not only to paternalistic traditionalists but also to inclusive-language genderphobes that things have never been quite as good as the former, nor as bad as the latter seem to think. Indeed, the woman presented here by Jesus seems to possess, in the fullest possible measure, both masculinity and femininity. It may be stereotypically female work she's pictured as doing, but she does it with more than stereotypically male energy. This is no slip of a girl making two tiny loaves for her husband's pleasure. This is a *baker,* folks. Three measures *(sáta)* is a bushel of flour, for crying out loud! That's 128 cups! That's 16 five-pound bags! And when you get done putting in the 42 or so cups of water you need to make it come together, you've got a little over 101 pounds of dough on your hands.

Which leads me, as long as we are at the end of the parable anyway, to exegete it backwards. Take the "whole" *(hólon)* first. When Jesus says the *whole* is leavened, he's not kidding. The lump stands for the whole world. It's not some elite ball of brioche dough made out of fancy flour by special handling. And it's not some hyper-good-for-you chunk of spiritual fad bread full of soy flour, wheat germ, and pure thoughts. It's just plain, unbaked bread dough, and Jesus postulates enough of it to make it even handle like the plain old world it represents: that is, *not easily.* Indigestible in its present form, incapable of going anywhere, either to heaven or hell, except in a handbasket — and absolutely certain to wear out anybody, God included, who tries to deal with it — it is, if we dare rate such things, one of Jesus' parabolic triumphs: a perfect 100+, if there ever was one.

The note of the *catholicity* of the kingdom, therefore, stands as the major emphasis of this parable, and I will not wave it in front of you any more than I already have. But when you go back to the word *ékrypsen*, "hid," and spend some time on the obvious element of *mystery* it introduces, additional light begins to shine on both notes.

The hiding of yeast in a batch of dough is both more mysterious and more pervasive than any of the hidings Jesus has so far used to illustrate the kingdom. Seeds may disappear into the ground; but if you are willing to take the trouble to hunt and peck for them, you can conceivably get every last one of them back up and out of the field. Furthermore, even when they are thickly broadcast, there is still more of the field unsown than sown. But yeast? No way, on either count. Just as yeast enters into the dough by being dissolved in the very liquid that makes the dough become dough at all — just as there is not a moment of the dough's existence, from start to finish, in which it is unleavened dough — so this parable insists that the kingdom enters the world at its creation and that there is not, and never has been, any unkingdomed humanity anywhere in the world.

For by, with, and in the very fluids that make and restore creation — by the waters on whose face the Spirit moved, by the mist that watered Eden, by the paschal blood on the doorposts, by the blood of the covenant on Sinai, by the waters of Jordan in Jesus' baptism, by the blood and water from his side on the cross, and by the river of life in the New Jerusalem — the Word, who is the yeast that leaves not one scrap of this lump of a world unleavened, has *always* been hidden in his creation. He did not start being hidden in 4 B.C.; all he did in his time on earth was show us his face and tell us his name — and send us out to share that Good News with everybody.

And just as the yeast, once it is in the dough (unlike the seed, once it is in the ground), is so intimate a part of the lump as to be indistinguishable from it, undiscoverable in it, and irretrievable out of it, so is the kingdom in this world. Indeed, this image of the perpetual intimacy of yeast to dough leads to a refinement of the notion of the kingdom in these parables. I have been saying that the kingdom is the *very thing sown,* not something that results from the sowing of a different thing. But now I can take it further. If the kingdom is like *yeast hidden in dough,* then we should stay well away from even the apparently harmless assertion that the kingdom is the yeast and the world is the dough. If the world *alone* (the world without the kingdom) is represented by anything in the parable, it is by the flour, not the dough. But in the action of the parable, the flour is never portrayed as alone. Rather, it is portrayed as dough with the yeast already hidden in it. Consequently, what the kingdom is actually represented by is the yeast-in-the-dough, the dough-cum-leaven — just as, when you come to think of it, the kingdom in the "seed" parables is most fully represented by the seed-in-the-ground, not simply by the seed alone.

Finally (under this same heading of the hiding of the yeast), I find that I can put my case even more strongly than I have so far for both the pervasiveness and the actuality of the kingdom's working in the world. It is all too tempting, after hearing the "seed" parables, to envision a time (namely, before the sowing) when the world was a world without the kingdom in it. (That tends to make hash of a serious view of the Old Testament, of course, and it makes no sense at all of the Word's intimate presence to the world as the one by whom all things were, and are, made;

nevertheless, it's still a temptation.) But after hearing the parable of the Leaven, there is no choice: for every second of the time the dough is dough, the yeast is inseparable from it. Therefore, for every second of the time the world has been a world, it has also been the kingdom. Its progress through history is not a transition from nonkingdom to kingdom; rather, it is a progress from kingdom-in-a-mystery to kingdom-made-manifest. (I know. You want to tell me it's at least possible to make a dough first and after that work the leaven into it. Don't bother. I'm a baker. Sure it's possible: I've done it. But it's also dumb: nobody in his right mind would choose to make bread that way unless he'd made a mistake to start with. And since this parable isn't about mistakes, I'm not about to allow them into my interpretation.)

Catholicity, mystery, and *actuality,* therefore, are in this parable in spades. But what about *hostility?* Obviously it is not here as such in any way; but there is one thing that heightens Jesus' admonition (in the parable of the Weeds) against taking up arms against it. Here, it is not simply that it is unadvisable or inconvenient or dangerous for us to interfere while the kingdom is doing its thing: it is plain, unvarnished impossible. So intimate is the yeast to the entire lump — so immediate is the working of the kingdom to every scrap of the world — that there is no way on earth of getting at it, or even to it, at all. Not for the enemy. Not even for the divine Woman Baker herself, apparently. And certainly not for any odd little bits of the lump like you and me.

And so we come at last to the note of *response* — and, fittingly enough, to the first image in the parable, that of the yeast. What are the only responses you need to offer to yeast-in-the-dough? Well, patience, for one thing. And possibly discernment — to be able to recognize when it (not you, please note) has done the job. And maybe a little vigilance to make sure impatient types don't talk you into despairing of the lump before its time comes. But no matter what you do, the yeast works anyway. At the most, your responses advance your satisfaction, not its success.

And even your negative responses — even your point-less resistances to the kingdom — interfere only with your own convenience, not with its working. Indeed, by the imagery of bread making, they may even help the kingdom. Unless the dough is kneaded thoroughly — unless it resists and fights the baker enough to develop gluten and form effective barriers to the yeast's working — then the gases produced by the yeast will not be entrapped in cells that can lighten the lump into a loaf. Who knows, therefore? Maybe even our foot-dragging and our backsliding — maybe even the gummy, intractable mass of our sins — is just all in a day's leavening to the Word who is the Yeast who lightens our lumpishness.

One last, first point about the *zýmē*, the leaven itself. How does yeast lighten dough? By filling it with thousands of tiny pockets of carbon dioxide. And how do those pockets of gas cause bread to rise? By expanding when heated. Behold, therefore, the way the imagery of the Leaven reflects and refracts Scripture's other references to warm carbon dioxide: that is, to *breath,* both human and divine.

The whole kingdom of God — the catholic, actual mystery that, come fair response or foul, is irremovably mixed into creation — operates by *warm breath*. It takes its origin from a Father's breathed-forth *Word* who, spoken once for all eternity, brings the world out of nothing into being. It marches through its history under the guidance of a *Spirit* — a *rúach,* a *pneúma,* a wind, a breath — who, proceeding from the Father's speaking of the Word, confirms that Word with signs following. And the imagery grows more and more complex. Jesus breathes out the Spirit upon his disciples after his resurrection. After he has ascended, he sends that same Spirit upon the church as a rushing mighty wind. And finally, when the church goes forth to announce the leavening of the world by all this trinitarian heavy breathing, it is by yet more warm breath — even by hot air — that the proclamation is made: "For after . . . the world by wisdom knew not God, it pleased God *by the foolishness of preaching* to save them that believe" (KJV, emphasis mine).

And do not try to cast a chill on the warmth of that Good News by telling me my last quotation means that the kingdom is at work only in "them that believe." To make belief the touchstone of the kingdom's operation is simply to turn faith into just one more cold work. Of course we must believe; but only because there is nothing left for us to do *but* believe.

All we need to do, and all we can do, is simply trust that the leaven is, was, and always will be entirely mixed into the lump of our existence — and that it will infallibly lighten every last one of us. The job is already, if mysteriously, done: by the power of the Word who breathed out his life for us on the cross — by the might of him who, in the glory of his resurrection, forever whispers our reconciled names into his Father's ear — we are as good as baked to perfection right now. We have been accepted in the Beloved; the only real development left for us to experience is the final accolade to be spoken over us by the divine Woman Baker: "Now *that's* what I call a real loaf of bread!"

CHAPTER TEN

The Interpretation of the Weeds

Even after the parables of the Mustard Seed and the Leaven, though, Matthew still seems unwilling to let Jesus proceed directly to an interpretation of the parable of the Weeds. At verses 34 and 35 of chapter 13, he inserts an editorial comment about Jesus' use of parables in general. The parallel passage in Mark occurs at 4:33-34, but since Mark omits the parable of the Weeds entirely, the function of these verses in his account is different than it is in Matthew. Coming as they do at the end of the Marcan collection of the parables of the kingdom, they serve principally as a coda on the parabolic method: "And with many such parables he spoke the word to them as they were able to hear it, but without a parable, he did not speak to them; privately, though, to his own disciples, he explained everything." Perhaps all that needs to be added here to what I said earlier about this text is a note of wonder: however marvelous the parables we possess may be, we simply don't have all of Jesus' parables.

Not that there is any point in speculating about why some (or many) were omitted: what might have been, wasn't — and that's all you can say about that. But the

124

comment does suggest an explanation for Jesus' popularity with the crowds. To us the Gospels display a Jesus who is, as often as not, a feisty character. This playing up of his contentious side has, no doubt, a simple explanation: Jesus was eventually done in by the hostility that surrounded him; therefore, the Gospel writers were at pains to explain its origin and development. The result, however, is that we easily forget the enthusiasm with which the crowds listened to him. He spoke colorfully, with surprising illustrations practically tripping over each other in his discourse. In a word, he was an entertainer as well as a teacher; by contrast, the scribes and Pharisees must have seemed like stuffed shirts.

But it is in the Matthean account that this editorial comment is given a positively fascinating twist. Matthew begins the passage more simply than Mark: "All these things," he says, "Jesus spoke to the crowds in parables; indeed, without a parable he said nothing to them." But then his Gospel-writer's mental concordance pops open at Psalm 78:2, and he cannot resist ringing the changes on the quotable passage he finds there. Jesus' whole use of the parabolic method, Matthew writes, has a scriptural precedent: he taught that way "in order to fulfill what was spoken by the prophet: 'I will open my mouth in parables [*en parabolaís*], I will utter things that have been hidden [*kekrymména*] from the foundation of the world [*apó katabolés kósmou*].'"

One note. I am about to comment here only on Matthew's mental concordance and on some other New Testament uses of the Greek words it flushed for him. Neither the meaning of the original Hebrew in the Psalm (probably something like, "I will utter dark sayings from of old"), nor the adequacy of the Greek version Matthew quoted from (for example, *kekrymména* is not in the Septuagint; rather, *problēmata* is), nor the state of the Greek text of the Gospel (*kósmou,* "of the world," is omitted from a few of the best and oldest manuscripts) — none of these things, interesting or even important though they might be, enters into my case at all. My argument goes simply to the reasons why Matthew included the passage at this point, and to what we can conclude, in the light of those reasons, about the parables of the kingdom in particular.

Fair enough then. Why Matthew's mind went to Psalm 78:2 in the first place is quite obvious: he had already written the phrase *en parabolaís,* "in parables," at verse 34; its occurrence in a psalm he probably knew from memory no doubt made it leap right out at him. Having gotten that far, however, he naturally proceeded to recite a bit more of the psalm; and that, finally, was what decided him on quoting the passage. For right there — right after he had just finished writing the parable of the Leaven and using the word *enékrypsen,* "hid," to describe what God does with the kingdom — there, plain as day, is the same root *kryp* hidden away in *kekrymména.* The psalmist, Matthew thinks, really was a prophet who anticipated Jesus' emphasis on hiding and even extended it backwards in time: the kingdom is not something that God will send at some future date to a world that is presently without it; rather, it is a real and operative mystery that God has *long since* encrypted in the world.

But it is as he recites the verse to its end that the reason for quoting it becomes overwhelming. These *kekrymména,* these hidden things, have been around a lot longer than just *since;* they have been here *apó katabolḗs kósmou,* from the foundation of the world. The mystery of the kingdom, therefore (if I may take over from Matthew at this point), has never *not* been in the world — just as the yeast that the woman dissolves in the water to make the dough has never not been in the lump. Because the creative Word is the eternal contemporary of every moment of the world's existence, the kingdom is catholic in time as well as space. The Word who restores humanity to its status as a kingdom of priests is the same Word who made Adam a priestly king to begin with. To be sure, since those first days in Eden, the kingdom has indeed been hidden and only the *signs* of the mystery (the people of Israel, the humanity of Jesus, the holy catholic Church) have been visible. But it has only been hidden, not absent; it has never once been something merely *yet to come.*

And therefore (to hand the wheel back to Matthew), it is finally safe, the Gospel writer thinks, to set down Jesus' interpretation of the parable of the Weeds. Having at last gotten the point across that, whatever things there may be still to come, the kingdom itself isn't one of them — having characterized it, once and for all, as *here* — he decides that maybe now a little eschatology wouldn't do too much damage.

Which brings us, naturally, to Matthew 13:36-43. The interpretation that Jesus gives of the parable of the Weeds in these verses is a flatfooted allegorization. Point by point, he ticks off a list of almost completely obvious correspondences between the details of the agricultural tale he has told and the details of the kingdom's contest with evil. Ordinary readers, of course, have found it not only acceptable, but gratifying: it's always nice when the teacher's explanations jibe neatly with the pupil's guesses at his meaning. But biblical critics have almost always been driven up the wall by it.

Many of them have felt that the interpretation is simply inauthentic — an ecclesiastical gloss poked into the text by some third-rate mind whose forte was beating people over the head with the self-evident. Others, though — more firmly committed to the notion that the canon of Scripture is, after all, the canon of *Scripture* — have soft-pedaled it in a different way: Jesus, they claim, was either having an off day when he unburdened himself of it, or else he gave it so early in his teaching career that his subsequent top-drawer parabolic style never had a chance to inform it. Whichever way they argue, though, they agree on one thing: the interpretation of the Weeds doesn't fit their specifications for an important piece of parabolic discourse.

Everybody, I think, can sympathize to a certain extent with their reservations. This allegorization of the parable is, after all, a bit trite; and it is even more than a bit premature. Follow up that last point. Jesus, in this passage, takes a parable that was only tangentially about the eschatological solution to the problem of evil and turns it into a full-fledged parable of judgment. Most of Jesus' parables of judgment, however, come much later in the Gospels than this; in fact, many of the most significant ones occur, as I noted in chapter 4, during Holy Week — that is, when Jesus' forthcoming passion and death were uppermost in his mind. In other words, his judgment parables tend to be more "hot" than "cool." They are not abstract treatises on the theology of the last things; rather, they are vivid stories told by a totally committed dying Messiah who is also wrestling with the obvious fact of the rejection of his sacrifice by nearly everyone around him.

Still, understandable though all those reservations may be, I don't like what the critics usually do with them. Enter here, therefore, my "dog biscuit" theory of Jesus' interpretation of the Weeds.

On a number of occasions, Jesus does and says things that I think are best understood not as his own considered opinion of what is called for in the circumstances but as sops for those he is dealing with. Consider the following. The healing of the demoniac boy (Matt. 17:14-23): Jesus' disciples can't cast out the demon; the boy's father pesters Jesus to cure him; Jesus answers, "O faithless and perverse generation, how long do I have to put up with you?" — and then he heals the boy anyway. Or consider the wedding at Cana (John 2): Jesus' mother tells him they have no wine; he says, "What have I got to do with you, woman? This isn't my time" — and then he turns water into wine. And there are plenty of other instances: the coin in the fish's mouth (Matt. 17:24) is best understood as a half-serious, throwaway miracle to shut up the yapping of the tax authorities; the raising of Lazarus (John 11) has the same "bone tossed to the dogs" element in it (Jesus is irked, *enembrimé-sato*, and upset, *etáraksen heautón*, at the prospect of having to do it just "on account of the crowd hanging around"); and finally, in Mark 7:27, Jesus actually refers to throwing things to the dogs. His calling the Syrophoenician woman a dog is part of an "in" joke between himself and her; the real dogs — to whom the bone of the healing of her daughter is thrown to spite them — are those whose superorthodox theology said the Messiah would never have any truck with Greeks.

But enough. To me, Jesus' allegorization of the Weeds — his terse tossing off of a straight "judgment" interpretation of a fundamentally nonjudgmental parable — is just one more dominical dog biscuit. His hearers have been itching to hear eschatology, so — mostly, I think, to get them off his back — he gives them eschatology. And eschatology that insults whatever intelligence they may have had. "O . . . kay," he says to them. "You're dying to mess up my point, so I'll mess it up for you. That way you get two parables for the price of one: the first is mine; but this second one is all yours. Chew on it all you like. Maybe some day it'll dawn on you it's not exactly the world's best bone."

To come to the text itself, then, note first that as Matthew sets up the passage, this last putative crack of Jesus' is aimed at the disciples themselves. Leaving the crowd, Jesus comes to the house and the disciples approach him. "Explain to us the parable of the Weeds of the field," they say. Ah, how fearful and wonderful it must have been to be the teacher of such a brilliant collection of point missers. Behold how, even in their first framing of the question, they have managed to turn the parable into something else. Jesus told it as a story of a kingdom that was like a man who sowed good seed in his field and then had weeds sown in it by his enemy; but they heard it as a story about weeds, period. What he gave them was a judiciously balanced analogy of the complex relationship between good and evil; but what they received was an out-of-whack fable about the problem of evil alone.

To give them credit, they did at least have a suspicion they hadn't quite understood his meaning. But to give Jesus even more credit, he probably realized that if they didn't get his first comparison, they wouldn't get any subsequent ones either. Therefore, anticipating Chesterton by 1900 years, he simply said, "Yes, you don't understand," and told them only what they were prepared to hear. In short, he backed away from the difficult concepts of the catholicity, mystery, and present actuality of the kingdom and gave them the "take up the sword against the sword" theology he would spend his whole life negating.

Quite possibly, you find that too fast a shuffle. And quite possibly it is. But on the other hand, I have no compunction about offering it to you. My commitment to Scripture as the inspired Word of God — as a sacred deck of cards, not one of which may be discarded and not one of whose spots may be altered or ignored — in no way inhibits me from *playing* with Scripture. Better minds than mine have done it before. For example, *Crux muscipulum diaboli,* said St. Augustine: the cross is a mousetrap for the devil; and then he proceeded to work out the whole scenario of the Crucifixion in pure mickey-mouse, complete with the devil salivating over the prospect of Christ's demise, and then being caught in the trap of the Redeemer's death, and finally realizing, in the Resurrection, that he had been tricked by fake bait. So enjoy. Or don't enjoy. There'll be another hand of cards along in a moment.

I have commented already on most of the identifications Jesus makes in allegorizing the parable of the Weeds: the sower of the good seed is the Son of Man; the field is the world; the good seed are the sons of the kingdom; the *zizánia,* the "bad seed," are the sons of the evil one; the enemy who sows them is the devil; the harvest is the end of the world. In no more space than I have taken to write them down here, he skips blithely over the heart of his original parable and heads for the eschatological barn; what got a mere two-thirds of a verse in the first version is about to get fully half the total space in this one.

The angels, he says, are the harvesters. I am sorry: it may be one of the drawbacks of the way my mind works, but I cannot resist imagining that Jesus is simply on a roll here. Who cares who the harvesters are? Their identity is completely irrelevant to his parable. But having set himself to "explain" everything to this bunch of dummies, he cannot resist laying it on thick. Indeed, I am a little surprised, given his flair for irony, he didn't lay it on even thicker: the angels are the harvesters; the pitchforks they use to gather up the weeds are the seven cardinal virtues; the strings they use to bind them into bundles are the moral attributes of Deity; the wagon they use to cart them off is the chariot of the wrath of God; and the team that pulls the loathsome load is the four horsemen of the Apocalypse.

I take back my apology. Putting it that way convinces me of something: Jesus didn't need biblical critics to tell him he shouldn't allegorize parables; he knew instinctively not to do it. And when he did actually indulge in it, he did so with such a heavy hand that the results were almost as good as the famous spoofing allegorization some critic made up for the parable of the Good Samaritan: the man who fell among thieves is the human race; the Samaritan is Christ; the oil and wine are the two Testaments; the inn is the holy catholic church; the innkeeper is the Pope; and the two pence are the two major sacraments, baptism and communion. And when the critic was told he had omitted the beast on which the Samaritan transported the wounded man, he replied, "Oh right, the ass: the ass is the fellow who made up this interpretation of the parable."

Again, though, enough. The rest of Jesus' allegorizations make the point all by themselves. "Just as the weeds are gathered and burned with fire," he says, "so will it be at the end of the age. The Son of Man will send his angels, and they will gather out of his kingdom all causes of sin [*skándala*] and doers of iniquity [*poioúntas tēn anomían*]."

Yes. That is indeed, in all seriousness, what God will do: it would be a pretty poor New Jerusalem that couldn't manage to get such menaces off the streets. But yes, again: Jesus' extensive dwelling on it here is still a dog biscuit thrown to the disciples to get himself shed of their simplistic eschatology. For between the ultimate cleanup of evil and his disciples' plausible but misguided eagerness to get their version of it going in high gear right now, he has yet to interpose the dark, mysterious, incomprehensible, unsatisfactory *áphesis* of his death, resurrection and ascension — the *letting be* of his redeeming, reconciling work that is both forgiveness and permission at once. Evil will be dealt with, but in no way as unparadoxically as they think: even hell — in the light of the general resurrection — is a kind of *áphesis,* an eternal *suffering* of evil. "So go ahead and think all you want about the scandals and the bad guys for the time being," he seems to say to them; "but you'd better hold onto your hats when you finally see what I'm going to do about them between now and the time to come."

All of that goes unmentioned, though: Jesus simply continues to heap up mocking reinforcements of his disciples' eschatological naïveté. "And they will throw them into the furnace of fire, *eis tēn kámiñon tou pyrós* [straight out of Nebuchadnezzar; by Daniel; Shadrach, Meshach, and Abednego, up] where there will be weeping and gnashing of teeth." Loud cheers from the apostolic band; the enemies of the Lord are getting it in the neck. God's in his heaven and all's as wrong as it possibly can be in hell. The saints look down and laugh themselves silly over the agonies of the damned. "Hurrah for justice! We knew God would finally see it our way — we who will be the righteous shining like the sun in the kingdom of our Father. What a wonderful way to end such a satisfying interpretation! Oh, thank you, Jesus; thank you very, very . . ."

But Jesus doesn't end there. He adds one final, devastatingly ironic note: *He who has ears, let him hear.* "You like all that eschatological vengeance, huh?" he says to them. "Well, keep listening, kiddies, because while it's true enough in its plausible little way, there are going to be so many other implausible truths before you get to it, you may not even recognize it when you see it. You've still got a lot more to take in."

CHAPTER ELEVEN

The Treasure and the Pearl

The next two parables of the kingdom — the Treasure Hidden in the Field and the Pearl of Great Price (Matt. 13:44-46) — are simply dropped without ceremony into the account. With no preface at all, Matthew writes: "The kingdom of heaven is like a treasure hidden [*kekrymménō*] in a field [*agrō*], which a man found and hid [*ékrypsen*]; then in his joy [*apó tēs charás autoú*], he goes and sells [*pōleí*] whatever things he has and buys [*agorázei*] that field. Again, the kingdom of heaven is like a merchant in search of fine pearls, who, on finding one pearl of great value [*polýtimon*], went and sold [*pépraken*] all that he had and bought [*ēgórasen*] it." I propose to exegete these two parables in one breath, as it were, and to do so by commenting on the Greek words I have flagged in the text.

First take the word *kekrymménō*, "hidden." It is a participle of the verb *krýptein*, which, in addition to its already noted appearances in the parable of the Leaven and in the quotation from Psalm 78 in Matthew 13:35, turns up in a number of other places where it underscores the note of the mysteriousness of the kingdom. In Matthew 11:25, Jesus says — referring to the unrepentant cities that paid no attention to the mighty works by which he was proclaiming the kingdom — "I thank you, Father, Lord of heaven and earth, that you have hidden [*ékrypsas*] these things from the wise and learned and revealed [*apekálypsas*] them to babies." Not even brilliant specialists in plausibilities, he insists, can discern the kingdom at work in their midst; only the mystery-loving simplicity of children can recognize its hidden reality.

Again, in Luke 18:31-34 — when Jesus foretells his death and resurrection for the third time — the Gospel writer notes that even at this point the twelve "did not understand any of these things, and this word was hidden [*kekrymménon*] from them, and they did not know what he was talking about." The mystery, in other words, even when its literal details are spelled out in so many words, remains inaccessible to anyone's understanding. Finally, in two other non-Gospel citations, the root *kryp* is used in direct reference to the mystery of redemption. In Revelation 2:17, he who stands in the midst of the seven lampstands says to the church in Pergamum, "To him who overcomes, I will give some of the hidden [*kekrymménou*] manna"; and in the most pregnant reference in all of Scripture, Paul tells the still-living Colossian Christians, "You have died, and your life is hidden [*kékryptai*] with Christ in God. When Christ, your real life, appears, then you too will appear with him in glory" (Col. 3:3-4).

Taken together, therefore, these passages give the full force of the hiding of the mystery. It is by no means some merely invisible proposition that won't bother you if you don't bother it; rather, it is the chief constitutive principle of the whole creative-redemptive order — and it is present in all its reconciling power whether you pay attention to it or not. The mystery, in short, is exactly what the parable of the Treasure hidden in the field says it is: something worth selling anything you must to enjoy possessing.

Consider next the word *agrō*, "field." We have already come across it many times in the seed parables, where it functioned as a surrogate for the whole world. In this parable, though, the note of catholicity is stood on its head, so to speak. Obviously, the treasure is not broadcast throughout the field; it is hidden in only one spot (or to be completely accurate, two spots: first, in the place where the man found it; and second, in the place where he himself hid it so he would have time to convert his nonliquid assets into purchase money). But the field Jesus speaks of here still has a fascinatingly catholic aspect: the smart businessman of the parable buys the *whole* field. Jesus' reference, therefore, is not to the catholicity of the mystery but to the catholic, you've-got-to-go-for-the-whole-deal kind of behavior that the mystery demands of those who choose to respond to it. The man in the parable, accordingly, is a surrogate not only for individual responses to the kingdom hidden in the world but also, and especially, for the church's response.

Every now and then at ecumenical gatherings, the Apostles' Creed is recited; and too often someone gets the kindly meant but misguided idea of substituting the words "holy Christian church" for "holy catholic church." In terms of the Gospel, that is a disastrous switch. The church is not, in any proper sense, Christian. Its members are indeed called Christians (though it is worth noting that the name was first applied to them, in Acts 11:26 and 26:28, by outsiders); but it is not some sectarian society whose members have a monopoly on the mystery. It is not a club of insiders who, because of their theology, race, color, or sex — or their good behavior, intelligence, or income bracket — are the only channels through which the Word conveys himself to the world. Rather, it is a sign to the world of the mystery by which the Light has already lightened the whole shooting match, by which the divine Leaven has already leavened the whole lump of creation.

Therefore, the church is precisely *catholic,* not Christian. It is not a sacrament to the few of a salvation that they have but the world does not. Rather, it is the chosen sign of the salvation of the entire world. And (to return to the purchase of the entire field by the man in the parable) the church has not only to "buy," to "deal with," the whole world; it must also, if it is to be any decent kind of sign at all, look as much like the world — and be as little different from the world — as possible.

Yes, I know. The church is indeed to be the salt of an otherwise bland earth. But that doesn't mean that the church itself is supposed to be *all* salt or that it is supposed to turn the world into *nothing but* salt. Therefore, when it represents itself to the world, it probably should not first of all be seen as salt. That's misleading advertising. You don't put dough-nuts in the window of a shoe store: that only confuses the public about your real business. Likewise you don't turn the church into a sodality that consists only of bright, white Anglo-Saxons who are happily married, have 1.8 children, and never get drunk. Instead, you just let it be what it in fact already is: a random sampling of the broken, sinful, half-cocked world that God in Christ loves — dampened by the waters of baptism but in no way necessarily turned into perfect peaches by them.

The church, like the purchaser of the field, can never afford to leave "unbought" any part of the earthly field in which God has hidden the treasure of the mystery. It does not dare to risk its own sure knowledge of where the mystery of the Word is — to risk its certainty that it has the right name of the Word (Jesus) and that it knows the precise location (the Incarnation) of the treasure that makes the whole world precious — by failing to purchase to itself every last bit of the field. The man who discovered the treasure did not simply buy the cubic yard or so of nice clean dirt in which he cleverly buried it. He bought the whole property: sinkholes, dungheaps, poison ivy, and sticker bushes, plus all the rats, mice, flies, and beetles that came with it. So too the church: if it can't bring itself to buy all sorts and conditions of human beings — white and nonwhite, male and female, smart and stupid, good and bad, spiritual and nonspiritual — it can't even begin to pretend it's catholic. Instead of being a sign of what the Word is up to in the world, it will become a sign of the very thing the Word is *not* up to, namely, the lightening of only some people, the sowing of less than the whole field, the leavening of two buns and a pretzel stick — and the discarding of all the rest.

But there is still more that can be said about the image of the field as this parable presents it. The treasure, clearly enough, is the mystery of the kingdom. The field in which it was buried, however, can be interpreted not only as the world but as the place in which, more than in all other places, the mystery's power lies hidden. It can be read, that is, as standing for *death*. Watch.

When we read this parable we automatically envision the treasure as buried underground in an otherwise wild or unused plot of land. Let me change the picture a bit, though. Since the parable mentions only a *hiding* of the treasure and says not a word about any burying of it, let me make the "field" an abandoned farm with a ramshackle farmhouse and an assortment of dilapidated barns and outbuildings. And let me further suppose that the prospective buyer, in checking over this not-too-promising addition to his holdings, first finds the treasure in a barn and then craftily moves it to the old henhouse for safe-keeping until the day when, having finally *bought the farm,* he can announce his phenomenal good luck at striking it rich.

138

Do you see? The phrase "bought the farm" (a euphemism for death, coined presumably by airline pilots whose demise would provide their wives with mortgage insurance to purchase outright their homesteads in Vermont) triggers a whole new set of meanings for this parable and give us yet another insight into the catholicity of the mystery. *We all buy the farm:* death, along with birth, is an utterly catholic experience. Some of us get rich; some of us get sick; some of us get funny in the head; some of us write books; some of us behave ourselves; and some of us live in Grand Rapids. But every last one of us dies. Willy-nilly, every single person in the world, Christian or non-Christian, will someday come into full and secure possession of the field of death in which Jesus has hidden the treasure of his redeeming work. And therefore, since no one, anywhere, at any time, will ever finally be without death, no one — on earth, in heaven, or in hell — will ever be without Jesus' reconciliation.

Oh, dear. I hear two objections. Let me interrupt myself to deal with them. The first is: "But hold on. Doesn't Scripture say that there will be some (or even many) who will reject the reconciliation?" Of course it does. But the very hell of hell lies precisely in the fact that its inhabitants will be insisting on a perpetual rejection of an equally perpetual gift. It will be an eternal struggle to escape from the grip of a love that will never let them go. And for that everlasting stand-off, I think, there is not a word in Scripture that is too strong: not the "fire that is not quenched," not the "worm that dieth not," not the "outer darkness," not the "bottomless pit," not the "weeping and gnashing of teeth" — and certainly not the utterly fruitless "second death."

The second objection is more trivial, but it leads to something far more profound. "First Thessalonians 4:15-

17!" the objectors howl: "We which are alive and remain unto the coming of the Lord shall not prevent them which are asleep. For the Lord himself shall descend from heaven with a shout, with the voice of the archangel, and with the trump of God: and the dead in Christ shall rise first: Then we which are alive and remain shall be caught up together with them in the clouds, to meet the Lord in the air: and so shall we ever be with the Lord" (KJV).

Pass over nearly everything about this text. Skip the question of whether it is enough of a foundation for all the pre- , post-, and amillennial theological architecture that has been piled on top of it. Forget about numbering the raptures. If you like, I'll sign my name to any eschatological scenario you want to write out. But in return, I want you to do me one favor: think just a little bit about the most likely historical circumstances under which your scenario will be played out. Unless the Lord mercifully cuts short the time — and cuts it very, very short indeed (like, say, down to tomorrow or the next day) — we will, by Murphy's law if nothing else, stage the end of the world for him with a nuclear holocaust. And while I'm sure God will have no theological problems with that (*any* end can serve as his end, just as *any* death, even the judicial murder of a common prisoner, can serve as his death), I'm equally sure that we who are alive and remain will have some serious practical problems.

In that day — when we are radiation-sick, ulcerated, bone-chilled, stupefied, and starving — whatever life we have left will make the dead look lucky. And whatever air there is to meet the Lord in will be death itself to breathe. Do you see? The glib and almost unpardonable effrontery of most eschatological hairsplitting fairly leaps out at you. To speak of two-bit theological distinctions in the face of a day like that is almost obscene — like making cool, theological small talk in the face of Jesus on the cross. For the fact is that the last day of this world — in the most likely script from which we will be allowed to act it out — is almost certainly going to be nothing less than the passion of literally everybody and the death of the whole earth.

So I hope you see why I have a certain profound impatience with quoters of 1 Thessalonians 4. This entire world is very nearly ready to buy the farm. Whether we meet the Lord in the air or not, there isn't one of us who will be saved by any other means than meeting the Lord in his death. *That* is the saving mystery; and one way or another, nobody is going to be excused from having the full force of it applied personally. Trouble me not, therefore: we are all going to be troubled to a fare-thee-well, and by experts.

But back to the parable. The next word, *ékrypsen,* brings up the second hiding of the treasure, this time by the very man who found it. I have said that the discoverer of the treasure stands for the church; does this rather shifty maneuver of his imply that the church may, under certain circumstances, hide the mystery? Well, not easily, I admit. It is hard to take an outfit supposedly operating under a charter to be a city set on a hill, a lamp not stuck under a bed, and make out a scriptural case that tells it to hide its message completely. But this parable suggests that a less radical hiding just might be a possibility. The man who found the treasure hid it so he could buy the field before anyone knew what he was really up to. He did not parade around beating people over the head with the news of his correct information about the treasure. He needed the whole field, so he acted in a way that would not jeopardize his eventual acquisition of it. So also the holy catholic church: its mission is to every single person in the world; therefore, it should not cut itself off from being heard by running around telling people where to head in before it even bothers to find out where they are coming from.

How many opportunities to proclaim the mystery has the church missed because it never took the time to learn the "language," cultural or historical, spiritual or practical, of the people it addressed? How often have the "un-churched" — the great catholic mass of unevangelized humanity who are, mind you, the very field in which the treasure of Jesus is already hidden, and who, but for their unbelief, would be enjoying him as mightily as believers do — how often have the unchurched put up a "not for sale" sign on their farm because they simply couldn't stand the arrogance of Christians?

And how much has the church itself missed? What treasures of understanding has it failed to buy? The Word that lightens everybody, everywhere, has been in business a long time. Not everything that "heathen" thoughts and deeds have produced came out of ungodly darkness. The wisdom of the East, for example, is not *all* foolishness, any more than the follies of Christians are all wise. But when the church approaches people as if God's whole, age-long, mysterious indwelling of the world had brought forth only two kinds of people — the utterly right and the totally wrong — then it deserves to have its money thrown back in its face. Whoever owned the field in the parable certainly wouldn't have sold it if the purchaser had shot his mouth off the way the church so frequently does.

But that is a very large subject indeed, so I simply leave it and return to the passage at hand. Consider next the word *pōleí,* "he sells," in verse 44, and the parallel word *pépraken,* "he sold," which occurs in the immediately succeeding par-able of the Pearl. *Pōleín and pipráskein* (to use the infinitive forms) are very nearly synonymous: both are used to refer to perfectly ordinary selling, and both have (as in the phrase "selling someone down the river") acquired the secondary sense of *betraying*. But *pipráskein* is also used for *selling into slavery* (e.g., Matt. 18:25 and Rom. 7:14), so it may have a bit more of an all-or-nothing flavor to it. At any rate, in the parable of the Treasure, the man simply sells *(pōleí)* "what things" *(hósa)* he has; but in the Pearl, the merchant sold *(pépraken)* "all things whatsoever" *(pánta hósa)* he had.

In "Little Gidding," the last of his *Four Quartets,* T. S. Eliot says that the only possible response to "the drawing of this Love and the voice of this Calling" is "A condition of complete simplicity/(Costing not less than everything)." The pearl is *polýtimon,* of great value, to the merchant, just as the treasure in the field was to the man who found it hidden; but both spent whatever they needed to make their purchases. The merchant of course, unlike the real-estate operator, was actually looking for fine pearls *(kaloús margarítas).* His discovery was not a lucky accident but the logical result of his being already and utterly committed to the pearl business. And what does that say about the catholicity of the mystery of the kingdom? Well, I think it makes yet another interpretive twist possible — one in which the world becomes the buyer, rather than the seller of the mystery.

All the children of Adam — all human beings, at all times, and in all places — are in the kingdom business, shopping night and day for the mystery of the city of God. Oh, true enough, like any random group of shoppers, they have their share of gullibility, questionable taste, and proneness to buy what's in the store rather than wait for what they're really looking for. But they *are* shopping. And they *are,* as often as not, quite willing to put their money where their heart's desire is. They are *not* simply a bunch of cheapskates; and they do *not,* given half a chance to see some first-rate goods, simply fob off the storekeeper with an "Oh, we're just looking."

Score yet another point, therefore, for the insistence that the church can safely afford to deal — indeed, that it dare not refuse to deal — with anything less than the whole world. It is catholic not only because the mystery it proclaims is already hidden everywhere but because the market for the mystery is a catholic market. The philosophies, religions, and mysticisms of the world — however bright or dim, kindly or cruel, lofty or loony they may be — are, as Paul intimated in the first chapter of Romans, evidence of a taste (albeit a sometimes perverted taste) for the truth. Show them the one pearl of great price, and they just might finally recognize it as the very thing they have been hunting for all along.

But the comparison says even more about the church's missionary enterprise. Not only should mission be entered into with full confidence that the world, wittingly or unwittingly, actually wants what we have to sell — and not only should we put the news of its high price as winningly as possible — we should also not be too quick to insult their taste in pearls before they get to our shop. And we should be equally slow to scare them out of the store with a lot of negative talk either about high prices or about the awesome, burdensome responsibilities incurred by those who acquire top-of-the-line merchandise. Of course there are responsibilities. Buying the world's finest pearl means guarding it and worrying about it and paying monstrous insurance premiums on it. But first and above all, it means actually owning the world's finest pearl — which, if you have even a smitch of a taste for pearls, has got to be a real "up."

How sad it is, then, to reflect on what the world actually hears from the church in so many instances. We offer to sell them the mystery of the love of God in Jesus; but the way we talk about God and Jesus only makes it sound as if we are trying to peddle a live rattlesnake. People converted by fear-mongering are people converted *from* evil, not *to* the truth. And if they ever work up enough nerve to make friends with the evil, woe to the missionary enterprise: the truth will be as if they had never bought it. If the merchant had bought the pearl only because he was afraid his friends would despise him if he hadn't, then the minute he got strong enough to tell his friends to fly a kite, he would have sold the pearl and bought something else.

All of which, I suppose, makes the Pearl a parable about a lot of the conversions in the history of the church. The mystery has been sold at spearpoint, at gunpoint, and at economic pressure-point; and such hard sells have even been justified on the basis of the mystery's catholicity: "It's good for everybody in the world," the church has said in effect, "so who cares how we get them to buy it?" But the mystery is a mystery of love and wants nothing less than a free offering of complete simplicity. If it waited for aeons even to show its face, it can certainly wait a few more days, months, or years for people to decide they actually like its name.

Which brings us to the last of the flagged words in the text, the verb *agorázein*, "to buy." Purchasing — and purchasing gladly, at whatever cost — is the point of both of these parables. Indeed, in the case of the treasure, it is precisely *apó tēs charás autoú*, out of his joy at the prospect of its possession, that the man sells the things he owns. For if the treasure and the pearl can be said to stand for the mystery — and if (to return to my original identifications) their unnamed owners can be said to stand for the church, and if the man in the first and the merchant in the second can be said to stand for the unevangelized world — then the buying of both the field and the pearl must be made to stand for nothing less than the ecstatic enjoyment of a *polýtima*, an utterly precious mystery that would have been cheap at twice the price.

The woman who walks out of Bendel's with a $15,000 mink and the man who pulls into the driveway with a brand-new, cream-and-gold Rolls Royce Corniche are not, in that moment at least, gloomy characters. And to bring the parable full circle, neither are the salespeople who closed the deals on such fabulous purchases. There is *joy* in heaven over one sinner that repents, not a lot of handwringing and brow-furrowing, and certainly not a boring "watch your step now" lecture from the divine counterparts of Bendel, Rolls, and Royce.

Therefore, there should be at least smiles in the church over the same happy turn of events. Not because we have made a buck, and not, God forbid, because we have compassed sea and land to make a proselyte; but only because the customers are satisfied — because they have put on the mink of righteousness, sat down in the Rolls Royce of salvation, and are now just laughing themselves silly over the incongruous wonderfulness of it all.

CHAPTER TWELVE

The Net

The parable of the Net, like Jesus' interpretation of the parable of the Weeds, is a story about judgment. But because it is also the last of the parables of the kingdom, I propose to reverse field and expound it in a way that postulates no irony whatsoever in Jesus' mind. Its very ultimacy suggests to me that my "dog biscuit" theory should be kept in the box this time around: Jesus himself, I think, quite seriously meant the Net to be a parable of judgment.

Authors commonly try to end their sections or chapters with items that provide a fitting climax to what went before. Accordingly, I am going to assume that either Jesus or Matthew (neither of them slouched when it came to authoring) did just that by ending the sequence of kingdom parables with the Net. For two reasons. The first is that its reference to the *synteleía tou aiốnos,* the completion, the end, the wrap-up of the age, makes it a natural as a finale. The same phrase, of course, occurs in the interpretation of the Weeds; but since that passage was placed more or less in the middle of the kingdom section, I felt freer to deal with it obliquely. But its occurrence here makes me want to give its eschatological points as much weight as they will bear.

The second reason follows from that. Whether this parable occurs last because Jesus habitually wound up his early, "kingdom-story" sessions with it, or because Matthew, as his editor, felt that logic called for it to be put at the end — whichever was the case, my commitment to the inspiration of Scripture leads me to believe that the Holy Spirit had his finger firmly in the pie. *All* of this parable's salient points, therefore — whether about judgment or anything else — should be examined with an eye to the way they sum up the picture of the kingdom so far. The Net is the final parabolic pass at the notes of catholicity, mystery, and so on, under which I have organized my exposition. I am curious to see if I can detect what the Spirit may have meant by this last move.

To begin: the net is a *sagéne,* a dragnet, a seine. ("Seine," by the way, is actually derived, via Latin and French, from *sagéne.* Even more interestingly, *sagéne* is what textual critics call a *hapax legomenon,* i.e., a word that occurs only once in the New Testament.) There are also two other words for "net" in the Greek text: *amphíblēstron,* "throw net," which occurs twice; and *díktyon,* the general word for "net" and "net-work," which occurs twelve times. But *sagéne,* appearing as it does only in this passage, is a particular kind of net, namely, one that is dragged through the water, indiscriminately taking in everything in its path. Accordingly, the kingdom of heaven (and by extension, the church as the sacrament of that kingdom) manifests the same indiscriminateness.

First reflection, therefore: As the net gathers up everything in its path — not only fish but also seaweed, flotsam, jetsam, and general marine debris — so too the kingdom gathers up everything in its path. Our usual mental image, of course, depicts the net as containing nothing but fish. Moreover, since the most obvious referent of the fish is people, we commonly suppose that the kingdom deals only with human beings. But in fact, the net of the kingdom touches everything in the world: not just souls, but bodies, and not just people, but all things, animal, vegetable, and mineral. In the context of the kingdom, for example, *Nero* is not just a dead Roman emperor; he is also a pet dog named to insult the memory of a persecutor of the kingdom. And hot cross buns are not just bread; they are the fruit of the plains marked with the sign of the mystery of the kingdom. And to come to a final, weightier illustration, gothic cathedrals are not just rock piles or shelters from the weather; they are stone parables of the splendor of the kingdom.

Accordingly, the note of catholicity is once again present in this parable, but with its range of meaning still further extended. Not only is the whole human race gathered into the kingdom; the entire physical order of the world is also drawn into it by the mystery of the Word. "I, if I be lifted up," says Jesus in John 12:32, "will draw *all* to myself." One note: Some texts read *pántas,* "all people"; others read *pánta,* "all things." The textual evidence leans in the direction of the former; but the latter remains at least a possibility. And that possibility, please note, is mightily enhanced by the imagery of the Book of Revelation: animal, vegetable, and mineral creatures throng the new earth as well as the old. There is a veritable bestiary of remarkable beasts; there is the tree of life in the New Jerusalem; and there is, at the center of it all, the city that lieth foursquare, the poetry of whose stonework makes even medieval cathedrals look like sand castles. In any case, just as the net fetches out everything it meets in the sea, so the kingdom fetches home to God everything in the world. The new heavens and the new earth are not replacements for the old ones; they are trans-figurations of them. The redeemed order is not the created order forsaken; it is the created order — all of it — raised and glorified.

But that is to get ahead of the story: this seine, this *sagéné,* Jesus says, gathers "of every kind" *(ek pantós génous).* It is fascinating that nowhere in this parable does the word "fish" actually occur. Naturally enough, we (along with most translators) automatically supply it as we read, and perhaps that is just what Jesus had in mind. But since it is not there, it occurs to me to make something of its absence. In line with that, I have already enlarged the contents of the net to include other things besides fish; let me simply ask you to bear that inclusion in mind as we go along. It will, I think, cast considerable light on the whole parable.

Right now, though, I want to concentrate on the phrase "of every kind." Obviously, it is a reference to the catholicity of both the net and the kingdom, but it is a reference that is a bit different from any made so far. In the parables of the Seed and of the Leaven, the emphasis was on the presence of the mystery of the kingdom to the whole world. But in this parable the emphasis is narrower: it is on the presence of *all the variety in the world* to the mystery of the kingdom. The parts of the sea through which the net was not dragged do not enter into the case in this parable; we are simply assured that, whatever kinds of things there may have been in the sea — good, bad, or indifferent — every kind is represented in the net.

Far more important, though, the parable does not rush into the business of judging between the various kinds. Consider: In the sea, all kinds of fish and all kinds of junk simply coexist. Before the net goes through it, there isn't even a hint of judging between good and bad, useful and useless. Indeed, the undragged sea, if it represented anything, would represent an unkingdomed world; but in the light of the other parables so far, there is just no such thing. In this parable, therefore, only the net-with-its-contents can fairly be said to represent the kingdom-in-the-world that the parables of the kingdom are at pains to portray.

But even that representation still does not introduce the note of judgment: neither the net as it makes its way through the sea, nor the kingdom as it makes its way through the world, can be said to reject anything. True enough, a sorting, a day of judgment, is clearly on the way in both cases, and once the eschatological shore has been reached, it will begin in earnest. But it does not take place before then. Therefore, neither the purse seine while still in the sea, nor the kingdom while still in this world has any business setting itself up in the judging business. And neither, a fortiori, does the church.

Which leads to a second reflection: if the kingdom works like a dragnet, gathering every kind, the church, as the sacrament of the kingdom, should avoid the temptation to act like a sport fisherman who is interested only in speckled trout and hand-tied flies. In particular, it should not get itself into the habit of rejecting as junk the flotsam and jetsam of the world — the human counterparts of the old boots, bottles, and beer cans that a truly catholic fishing operation will inevitably dredge up. Because while the kingdom itself will indeed make it onto the eschatological beach, the church, as now operative, will not. The church is only the sacrament of the kingdom — a visible sign of a presently invisible mystery. But in the Last Day, the church as such will not be necessary at all; the mystery of the kingdom will stand revealed in and of itself and will need no sacraments or signs whatsoever.

The church, in short, has a role to play *only here and now;* so if it wants a role model for its operations, it should imitate the kingdom's present, nonjudgmental way of doing business, not its final one. It definitely should not attempt, in this world, to do the kind of sorting out that the kingdom so plainly refuses to do until the next.

But alas, beginning right in apostolic times — indeed, beginning even in Scripture itself — excommunication has been one of the church's favorite indoor sports. Second only in popularity to jumping to conclusions about who should be given the heave-ho first, the practice of tossing out rotten types while the net is still in the water has been almost everybody's idea of a terrific way to further the kingdom. Everybody's, that is, except Jesus' — the one who put the church in the business of being fishers of men to begin with. The net result, to use an apt phrase for such ineptness, has been an operation that looks as if it is being run more by his competitors than by his partners.

Jesus didn't shy away from sinners, so why should the church? And don't tell me the church welcomes sinners. I know better. It welcomes only sinners who repent and then never seriously need forgiveness again. It can reclasp to its bosom members who gossip or lose their tempers (*little-bitty* sins, apparently — though where that qualification came from is not clear); but God help those who fornicate or lose their will to stay married. And it has the gall to make such invidious distinctions in the name of a Lord who unqualifiedly told Peter, the Chief Fisherman, to forgive his sinful brother (Andrew, perhaps? — maybe he wasn't the good old boy he was cracked up to be) seventy times seven times.

"Ah, but," you object. "What about *reform*? Are we to give the world the impression it doesn't need to straighten up and fly right? Are we simply to imply that it can get away with murder if it likes?"

Well, for openers, the world has already gotten away with — no, that's too weak; it has already been absolutely saved by — its murder of God himself incarnate. But for closers, neither the world nor the church has ever had much more than the glide angle of a coke bottle. Sure, there is the power of the Holy Spirit to make people better. But note carefully that that's not what you were talking about when you broke in with your objection. You were talking about what *we* should or shouldn't do to improve the human race's aeronautics. And about that, I have only one thing to say: "If there had been a law given that could have given life, verily righteousness should have been by the law. But the scripture hath concluded all [*ta pánta,* fascinatingly, "all *things*"] under sin, that the promise by faith of Jesus Christ might be given to them that believe" (Gal. 3:21-22, KJV).

Do you see? If even the divine jawboning on Mount Sinai couldn't reform the world, why should we think that our two-bit tirades against sin will do any better? So once again: sure there's reform; and it is even an important subject. But like everything else about the kingdom, it works in a mystery: it comes not when we decide to enforce it but only when God, by his paradoxical power, brings it about in his own implausibly good time. If he is willing to wait for it, why should the church be in such a rush? After all, it is *his* fish business we are supposed to be in.

Eventually, though (to return to the parable), Jesus does indeed get around to the subject of judgment. The fishermen did three things when the net was finally full: they hauled it up on the beach; they sat down; and they gathered *(syn-élexan)* the good *(ta kalá)* into a bucket and threw the bad *(ta saprá)* away. Time for a full-scale halt: I have deliberately given faulty translations for all of those Greek words.

First, *synélexan,* "they gathered." The verb *syllégein* is used seven times in the New Testament. Four of those uses occur in the parable of the Weeds and its interpretation (Matt. 13:29, 30, 40, 41) in connection with the gathering

153

up of the *zizánia* (weeds), the *skándala* (things that offend), and so on; the other two uses occur in Matthew 7:16 and its parallel, Luke 6:44 ("Do men *gather* grapes of thorns or figs of thistles?"). Translators have been divided over how to render the word: their versions have ranged from the quite clearly judgmental "sort out" to the almost neutral "collect." On balance, though, "sort" has perhaps the best claim — especially when it comes to translating a parable of judgment.

The words "the good" and "the bad," however, are much more dubious translations. *Kalós* in Greek does indeed mean "good," but with overtones of "beautiful," "fine," or "fair"; it is not as narrowly moralistic as the other common Greek word for "good" *(agathós)*. Jesus, for example, calls himself "the good shepherd" *(ho poimén ho kalós)*, implying, presumably, that he is something more than just an ethical shepherd — that he is, in fact, an admirable one, even an extravagantly beneficent one. Still, *kalós* and *agathós* are often used more or less interchangeably for both moral and aesthetic (or utilitarian) goodness, so I want to put only a blunt, rather than a fine point on the distinction.

Saprós, though, is another matter. Like most languages, Greek bears witness to the wretched state of human nature by having more words for badness than for goodness. *Kakós* is perhaps the most common word for "bad." But there are plenty of others: there is *ponērós*, "evil"; *ánomos*, "lawless"; *áthesmos*, "unsettled"; *phaúlos*, "worthless"; and there is, of course, *saprós*: "rotten, putrid, corrupt, worthless, useless." *Saprós* appears in five passages, four of which show its obvious suitability for use as the ugly opposite of *kalós*. Consider, for example, Matthew 7:17 (which displays, along with the opposition of *kalós* and *saprós*, some other twists and turns of the Greek "good/evil" vocabulary): "So every good [*agathón*] tree bringeth forth good [*kaloús*] fruit; but

a corrupt [*saprón*] tree bringeth forth evil [*ponēroús*] fruit"
(KJV). Or for an even clearer illustration of the opposition
of *kalós* and *saprós,* consider Matthew 12:33: "Either make
the tree good [*kalón*] and his fruit good [*kalón*]; or else
make the tree corrupt [*saprón*] and his fruit corrupt [*saprón*]"
(KJV). (The remaining passages, by the way, are Luke 6:43,
parallel to Matt. 12:33, and Eph. 4:29, where *saprós* is
contrasted with *agathós.*)

What can be said, therefore, about the sorting of the
contents of the net into *kalá* and *saprá*? Well, let's talk first
as if the net contained only fish. If that were the case, the
sorting might be based on a variety of considerations. Quite
likely, it could involve a separation of desirable food species
from unacceptable "trash" species. Just as likely, it could
involve a separation of marketable big fish from un-
marketable small ones. Less likely, it could involve a dividing
of sickly, unacceptable specimens from healthy, desirable
ones. Least likely of all, it could involve the separation of
dead, putrid fish from live, sound ones. In any case, though,
the criterion is not the innate goodness or badness of the
fish themselves, but *their acceptability to the fishermen.* It is
their utility or their beauty, in short — their being found
kalá in the eye of the beholder — that lands them in the
"save" bucket. And it is the judgment of *saprá* (rotten! ugly!
icky! crummy! yech!) that gets them thrown away on the
beach.

And the same thing is true if we postulate general marine
garbage as well as fish in the net. Whatever serves the
fishermen's purposes is kept; whatever does not is tossed
out. But notice an important element here: there is always
the possibility that some of the damnedest things might be
saved: old rusty anchors, bald tires, and broken lobster pots
might just make the cut if somebody took a shine to them.
In short, the net contains many things, but there is nothing,

however decrepit in and of itself, that absolutely has to be gotten rid of. Whatever sorting is done depends entirely on the disposition of the sorters. If they don't say "yech!" to something, then it's not *saprón*.

Admittedly, when Jesus comes to apply the imagery of this parable to the end of the world, he introduces another word for badness, namely, *tous ponēroús,* "the wicked," those who are willfully evil. But at the present point in the parable, that notion is simply not here. Reserving willful wickedness for later comment, therefore, I propose to press a little on this matter of the eye of the beholder being the key to the difference between *ta kalá* and *ta saprá*.

I have said that it is the fishermen, not the fish, who set the standards for the day of judgment on the beach. Therefore, it is the kingdom — and a fortiori, the King — who sets the standards for the Last Day of the world. But notice something peculiar about that day. It occurs, as I have already said, *after* the general resurrection: every last person who arrives at it arrives in the power of Jesus' reconciliation. The judgment, therefore, is first of all the announcement not of vindictiveness but of vindication. Everyone who comes before the Judge has already been reconciled by the dying and rising of the Judge. The only sentence to be pronounced, *as far as the Judge himself is concerned,* is a sentence to life, and life abundant.

Someone once said, "The world God loves is the world he sees in his only-begotten Son." If that is true, it means that at the last day, the whole world — the *all* that Jesus, in his being lifted up, has drawn to himself — is accepted in the Beloved. No one has to accept that acceptance, of course. It is entirely possible, both humanly and scripturally speaking, for anyone to thumb his nose at the reconciliation and try to go it on his own forever. And it is totally certain that if anyone wants to indulge in that kind of behavior, there is no possibility of keeping such a party pooper at the marriage supper of the Lamb. Hell is the only option for the finally recalcitrant.

But note well that nobody goes to hell because he had a rotten track record in the world — any more than anyone goes to heaven because he had a good one. Everyone, of every kind, who lands on the millennial beach has been fished up there by the net-work of the death and resurrection of Jesus. No one is judged by what he was like before that net caught him; the standards for the judgment are the divine Fisherman's standards, not those that were used to approve or disapprove of the fish as they formerly existed in the sea. And since those standards are one and the same as the divine Judge's, they are vindicative, not vengeful standards. We are not judged by our previous performances (on that basis, nobody would go anywhere but to hell); rather, we are judged by what Jesus did for us on the cross. He pronounces an authoritative *kalá* over the whole world that he has caught in the net of his reconciliation. It is only those who want to argue with that gracious word who are then pronounced *saprá*. Both heaven and hell are populated entirely and only by forgiven sinners. Hell is just a courtesy for those who insist they want no part of forgiveness.

And if the King wills finally to favor every last sinner with his reconciling *kalá*, how much more should the church — which is a sign to the world of his kingdom of forgiveness — pronounce the same *kalá* over the sinners with which it has to deal? Everybody, even the worst stinker on earth, is somebody for whom Christ died. What a colossal misrepresentation it is, then, when the church gathers up its skirts and chases questionable types out of its midst with a broom. For the church to act as if it dare not have any dealings with sinners is as much a betrayal of its mission as it would be for a hospital to turn away sick people or for a carpenter to refuse to touch rough-cut wood.

Sinners are the church's *business,* for God's sake. Literally. Let the scribes and the Pharisees — the phony-baloney, super-righteous, unforgiving scorekeepers who delight in getting everybody's number — take care of any judging that they want to: *judgment now* is their cup of tea, and they can poison themselves all they want with it. But let the church — which works for somebody who delights in getting everybody's *name* — stay a million miles away from it. We are supposed to represent a Lord who came not to judge the world but to save it. Our business should be simply to keep everybody *in* the net of his kingdom until we reach the farther shore. Sorting is strictly his department, not ours.

But on with the parable. After Jesus has set up the earthly imagery of his story, he turns to the task of applying it to the eschatological reality it stands for: "So will it be at the end of the age [*en tę synteleią tou aiōnos*]. The angels [*ángeloi*] will come and separate [*aphorioúsin*] the evil [*tous ponēroús*] out of the midst of the righteous [*ek mésou tōn dikaiōn*]."

Note first the word *syntéleia,* the end, completion, consummation, wrap-up. It stands not just for a denouement, a last unwinding, but for an arrival at something that has been in the works all along. *Télos,* the Greek root of the word, means "end, goal, purpose"; *syn* is a prepositional prefix meaning "with" or "together." *Tetélestai,* "it has been accomplished," was one of Jesus' last words on the cross; *tele*ology is the branch of philosophy that deals with the concept of *purpose.* This *syntéleia,* this wrap-up, then, is the final fruition of Jesus' work; and as such, it should be understood as of a piece with all the gracious rest of that work. It should not be propounded as a last-minute switcheroo that turns his entire redemptive ministry into nothing but a temporary — and deceptive — come-on.

Next, note what this *syntéleia* is the consummation of: it is the completion of *tou aiōnos,* "of the age," that is, of the whole history of the world. In older English versions, *tou aiōnos* is commonly translated simply as "of the world" (*aiōn* in Greek became *saeculum* in Latin, which in turn gave us "secular" in English: hence, "world" as a possible translation). But *aiōn* means far more than just the world as world or even the world as fallen creation: it means the entire historical process — good in some respects but fatally flawed in others — by which the world marches and/or stumbles toward its destiny. Once again, then, the note of *completion* creeps in. The world may have done its damnedest to reach what it considers its proper conclusion, but God in Christ has done his blessedest to take away the curse it put on itself in the process; now, at the *synteleía tou aiōnos,* at the final meeting of the blessing and the curse, he is about to make the blessing stick once and for all.

And how does he do that? Well, by George, he does it by *ángeloi,* by angels. In my comments on the interpretation of the Weeds, I dismissed the angels in that context with a "who cares who they are?" Let me take that back now. The angels stand for something of major significance here: fascinatingly, there is no strict counterpart to them in the first half of the parable of the Net as Jesus told it. It was the *fishermen* who did the sorting on the beach. The implication, therefore, was that the very same crew who dragged the net ashore would be the ones doing the job of separation. But when Jesus comes to the second half of the parable, he brings in a whole new crew, totally and irreversibly committed to doing only and always what *he* wants done. Do you see? "The Father . . . has committed all judgment to the Son" (John 5:22): nobody else — not the Father, not the Spirit, and certainly not the church — gets into the act. The job is strictly in the hands of Jesus and his utterly subservient heavenly bailiffs — which means, when all is said and done, just in Jesus' hands, period.

And what is it that these minions of his do? They "separate" *(aphorioúsin)*. They make no decisions; they implement no policies of their own; they simply move resurrected bodies around as directed by him who is the Resurrection and the Life. And on what basis, finally, does he direct them to make that separation? On the basis of his decision to get *tous ponēroús,* the evil ones, out of the midst of *tōn dikaiōn,* the righteous ones.

Time for another large-size halt. *Question:* How did those righteous ones get to be righteous? *Answer:* By the free gift of Jesus' righteousness. *Question:* To whom was that free gift offered? *Answer* (unless you believe in double predestination): to every human being who ever lived. *Question:* Do you actually mean that there's nobody at the Last Judgment who hasn't been given the righteousness of Christ? *Answer:* Yes, that's exactly what I mean. *Question:* Then how come some of them are judged *ponēroús? Answer:* Because even though they've got his righteousness, they've decided they don't like it; they can't stand the thought of not being accepted on their very own personal merit (which is one of the world's great nonexistent quantities, of course — but then, they seem to miss that point). *Question:* Wherever did you dig up ideas like this? *Answer:* Matthew 22:1-14. Any more questions?

This parable, you see, I take to be an honest-to-God parable of judgment, not just a dog biscuit. And therefore I am disposed to read it in the light of all the weightier parables of judgment that Jesus eventually told. Hence, Matthew 22:1-14. The fellow without the wedding garment in the parable of the King's Son's Wedding was precisely *ponērós:* he willfully balked at the one easily met condition of his attendance at the party. *Nobody* who was actually at the reception had a *right* to be there. Earlier in the story, of course, there were indeed people who deserved to be invited, but they had all refused the invitation — one going to his farm, another to his merchandise, and the rest of them murdering the king's servants. The ones who finally did get into the party were those who, despite their unfitness and their undeserving, were simply dragooned into attending. The indiscriminate dragooning, in fact, was the very thing that made them acceptable even in their unacceptableness; just as the catholic netting action of the kingdom is what proclaims the whole human race to be accepted in the Beloved. All the inhabitants of the world, in other words, are being drawn toward the final *kalá* that the Word wants to pronounce over them. Jesus does say, quite obviously, that if anyone doesn't like that ending of the story, he can lump it in outer darkness; but still, anyone who wanted to could have enjoyed it free-for-nothing.

There, then, is the force of *ponērós:* not just moral or aesthetic badness, but willful evil. The *ponēroús* whom the angels finally separate out of the midst of the righteous are not just *kakoús* (i.e., un-*agathoús* or un-good in a narrowly moral sense), and they are not just *saproús* (i.e., un-*kaloús* or un-good in the aesthetic or beautiful sense); they are positively and cussedly determined to reject Jesus' offer to ignore both their badness and their rottenness and to welcome them to the party anyway as *dikaíous,* that is, as clothed with his very own righteousness. They are, in short, ill-willed troublemakers. Like *ho ponērós* himself — like the evil one from whom we pray to be delivered in the Lord's Prayer — like the father of lies who hates the truth simply because he didn't invent it — they refuse to accept any gift, however gracious, unless they themselves are convinced they have an inalienable personal right to it.

And what, therefore, do the angelic bouncers do with

such maleficent, belly-aching types? They separate these *ponēroús* out of the midst of the righteous *(ek mésou tōn dikaíōn)*. In short, they pitch them out on their ear so they won't ruin the party. Even the eternal banishment of the wicked, you see, is a celebrative, vindicative judgment. There is to be *joy* in heaven not just over one sinner who repents but over the ninety and nine as well — over a whole New Jerusalem populated by nothing but sinners whose citizenship is based on nothing but their acceptance of forgiveness. If anybody doesn't want to be there on that basis, he can, quite literally, just get the hell out.

But then comes the end of the parable: "And they will throw them into the furnace of fire [*eis tēn káminon tou pyrós*]; out there [*ekeí*], there will be wailing and gnashing of teeth [*ho klauthmós kai ho brygmós tōn odóntōn*]."

The "furnace of fire," as I have noted, occurs at the end of Jesus' interpretation of the Weeds; it also turns up in another eschatological context, Revelation 9:2. But the "wailing and gnashing of teeth" occurs in a whole raft of such contexts: Matthew 8:12; 13:42, 50; 22:13; 24:51; 25:30; and Luke 13:28. In any case, each phrase has its unique force: the furnace suggests discomfort applied from the outside; the wailing and gnashing of teeth suggest anguish that springs from within. Not that there is much to choose between them; either would seem quite sufficient punishment for those who insist on being eschatological wet blankets. But taken together, the phrases bear witness to a double truth about the redeemed order: the furnace testifies to God's absolute insistence that nothing and nobody is going to rain on his final parade; and the wailing, to the equally absolute certainty that his parade is the only show in town that's going to be any fun. All that there is out there — in outer darkness — is an eternal, stinking pile of self-pity, festering its way to an equally eternal production of angry gas. The damned are not a crowd of wistful types, pining away for a wonderful deal that some mean scorekeeper of a God did them out of. They are a bunch of unreconstructed haters who threw away the best deal they were ever offered and now can't find anybody but themselves to be furious with.

It's not a pretty picture. But then, the *ponēroí* are not very pretty themselves. Still, except for their willful refusal of the reconciliation, they could have gone, just as easily as the righteous, from the net into the bucket. There was no compelling reason for them to spend eternity gasping on the beach.

Epilogue

Matthew's compendium of the parables of the kingdom — as well as my own treatment of them — ends with a passage (13:51-52) that, while parabolic enough, is not exactly a parable in the sense we have so far come to expect. Instead, it is a parabolic utterance of the sort we came across in the quotation from Psalm 78:2, that is, a "dark saying." And though it could easily be expanded into a narrative parable by any preacher who was willing to supply his own details, it is, as we have it, more a one-line comparison than a story.

Furthermore, it begins without any introduction. This has happened before (in the parables of the Treasure Hidden in the Field and in the Pearl of Great Price) but not quite as abruptly as here. Indeed, so absent is any clear pause for breath that this passage might logically be taken as a mere coda to the parable of the Net. Nevertheless, I find it makes even better sense as the capstone of the whole collection, so that is how I propose to read it.

"Jesus saith unto them," Matthew writes, "have ye understood [*synékate*] all these things [*taúta pánta*]?" (KJV). Note first of all that these words are not addressed to the crowds. Matthew, if you recall, has had Jesus in the house with his disciples ever since the beginning of the interpretation of the Weeds; it is the disciples, therefore, who respond to the question. "They say unto him, Yea, Lord [*nai, kyrie*]" (KJV).

And in response to that answer Jesus gives the parabolic summation of everything he has been saying about the mystery of the kingdom. "Then said he unto them, Therefore every scribe [*grammateús*] which is instructed [*mathē-teutheís*] unto the kingdom of heaven [*tḗ basileíą tōn ouranón*] is like unto a man that is an householder [*oikodespótę*], which bringeth forth [*ekbállei*] out of his treasure [*thēsauroú*] things new and old [*kainá kai palaiá*]." (This preliminary translation of the passage is taken verbatim from the KJV: since there are so many comments to be made about the flagged words, I want to start out on at least familiar, if not exactly unimpeachable, ground.)

To begin with, only the Byzantine manuscript tradition, plus a handful of other sources, has the words "Jesus says to them" at the beginning of the passage. They are omitted in the older manuscripts that make up the so-called Hesychian or Egyptian tradition, so most modern editors simply leave them out of the text and have Jesus begin directly with his question, "Have you understood all these things [*syné-kate taúta pánta*]?"

Synékate is from *syniénai*: to send, bring, set together. By extension, it also means to take notice of, know, understand. Accordingly Jesus is asking his disciples, "Do you grasp what I've been trying to tell you? Do you think you're able to put all this stuff together?" In spite of the disciples' track record for being slow on the uptake, he still seems to have his hopes: the crowds outside may have heard only odd, entertaining stories, but maybe this hand-picked, advanced class of insiders will do better.

If you have ever done any teaching, you know that it takes no small amount of courage for an instructor to ask such a question. Jesus has been at pains to expound a very different kingdom from the one his hearers, outsiders or insiders, were expecting. It is *catholic*, not limited just to the chosen people; it is paradoxically and vexingly *hidden*, not plausibly and gratifyingly manifest; it is *at work now*, not simply waiting for some future date; it operates in the midst of *hostility*, not welcome; and the *responses* it calls for are, hands down, the most mystifying propositions yet: not warfare, not haste, not a helping hand, not a quick, easy purchase, but rather nonviolence, patience, noninterference, and an investment the size of the national debt. It's a brave teacher who has the nerve to hope his pupils will have grasped even a tenth of such mind-boggling information.

Once again, if you have ever done any teaching you will understand that the answer Jesus gets to his question is not exactly encouraging. "They say to him, 'yes' [*nai*]." The Greek word, like the English one, can mean anything from a "Yes indeedy, we've taken in every last item, and we're ready to explain it at length to anybody who comes along," all the way down to an "Uh-huh," muttered chiefly in the hope that it will hoodwink the teacher into not asking them to recite. I am relatively certain that Jesus — who besides being a practiced pedagogue also "knew what was in man" — was quite clear in his own mind that it was the latter, rather than the former sense of *nai* that his disciples had in mind. In any case, it is a fact that they hardly understood him at all — and that they continued to misunderstand almost all of his deeds and words, parabolic or not, until well after his Resurrection.

The Byzantine manuscript tradition, incidentally — with its sometimes "churchy" overtones — corroborates this impression. In those manuscripts, the disciples say *nai, kyrie,* yes, Lord; they add a deferential "Herr Professor" to their affirmation as a further smokescreen for their incomprehension. Still, the older and better tradition leaves it at the almost-dumb *nai,* and so, accordingly, do most editors. The unvarnished "Uh-huh," has quite enough punch all by itself — a punch, in fact, that would hit any veteran teacher right in the solar plexus.

Jesus, however — pro that he is — doesn't even miss a breath. Plunging right ahead, treating his question as purely rhetorical so they won't have a chance to gum up the lesson with their own tacky explanations, he simply delivers his prepared last line anyway. "And he said to them, 'Therefore [*diá toúto*], every scribe [*pas grammateús*]. . . .'"

But stop there for a moment. *Diá toúto* means literally "on account of this"; but the disciples' "yes," as I have interpreted it, scarcely seems to provide much of an antecedent for the "this." Accordingly, it's hard to see how what he says next follows from their reply with any great logic. "On account of" seems entirely too strong; but even such translations as "therefore," or "this means, then," or "you can see, then," or even "well, then" (all of them used in various modern versions) seem overly consequential. What is needed, therefore, is a rendering that makes his next words a kind of two-way response — one that is a consequence of both their professed comprehension and their actual incomprehension at the same time. My own suggestion (admittedly just a tad colloquial, but expressing both gratification and skepticism) is this: "And he said to them, 'O–kay; then just listen: every scribe. . . .'"

Which brings us to *grammateús,* "scribe." *Grámma* in Greek means "letter," as in a letter of the alphabet. A *grammateús,* therefore, is a "lettered," that is, a "learned," person. The scribes (of the well-known team, scribes and Pharisees) were lay Jewish scholars of the four or five pre-

Christian centuries, and they are referred to (as *hoi gram-mateís*) some sixty or so times in the New Testament. In most of the references they are represented almost as a sect or a political party; but in a few places — this one in particular — that just may not be the case. In Matthew 23:34, for example, Jesus says, "Behold, I send to you prophets and wise men and scribes [*grammateís*]" — implying simply "learned men." In 1 Corinthians 1:20, Paul asks "Where is the wise man, where is the scribe [*grammateús*], where is the debate-enthusiast of this world?" — *grammateús*, once again, apparently referring more to just plain scholarship than to membership in a faction.

In this passage, therefore, it is quite possible that Jesus was using the words *pas grammateús* to mean "every one who has been instructed" in the kingdom of God — or even more narrowly, "every one who has received *my* instruction." Nevertheless, since the precise thing in which the scribes themselves were scholars was the Old Testament Law, the Torah — and since Jesus later refers to "things old" as well as "things new" — it is probably neither wise nor perhaps even possible to eliminate the notion of scribal Torah-learning from the word *grammateús* here. Hence the rather confusing field day that modern translators have had with this passage. Check out any number of them, and you will see that they are caught over several barrels at once: they want to get away from the usual, derogatory sense of "scribe," but they don't want to go so far in the direction of general scholarship that they lose the reference to the Torah altogether.

Probably, there is no satisfactory, simple solution to the problem: no single English word has all the shadings of *grammateús*. Perhaps the only workable approach is to abandon literal translation completely, as J. B. Phillips does, for example, and just toss in as many extra words as you may need to get the general idea across.

To an almost equal degree, the same difficulty plagues the translator of the phrase "instructed unto the kingdom of heaven" *(mathēteutheís tḗ basileíᾳ tōn ouranṓn). Mathēteutheís* means simply "taught," as in, "she has been taught how to cook." And *tḗ basileíᾳ* is simply the dative singular of *hē basileía,* the kingdom. It is used here, possibly, as a dative of relation ("taught the things *related* to the kingdom"), or possibly as a dative of interest ("taught *for* the kingdom"), or less possibly, perhaps, even a dative of agent ("taught *by* the kingdom").

At any rate, in the Greek, "kingdom" is simply a word in the dative case. The specific hairsplittings of the grammarians are not commonly uppermost in the minds of people who understand the language. Rather, when any particular grammatical usage is presented to them, they tend to hear not only its most natural sense but also as many of its additional shadings as the passage in question will bear. Therefore the following translations are all possibilities: "taught *for*," "taught *unto*," "taught *in relation to*," "taught *about*" — or even such periphrases as "has become a learner *in*" or "becomes a disciple *of*" the kingdom of heaven. Hence, once again, the bewildering variety of modern translations.

Nevertheless, Jesus' fundamental meaning seems fairly clear: "O–kay," he says, "you say you understand; so now I'll tell you something: every careful listener to what I've been teaching you about the kingdom of heaven is like a man who is an *oikodespótēs* [a householder]." The translation "householder," however, is a bit weak for *oikodespótēs* — and "homeowner," a more modern choice, is even worse. The Greek word (which comes from the roots *oik-,* house, and *despot-,* lord, master, slaveowner) means "house manager," or even "major domo." Therefore, what Jesus is saying to them seems closer to: "Once you've been taught about the

169

kingdom of heaven by me, you're going to be like someone who's been given full authority over an incredibly rich castle. There will be nothing you lack and nothing you'll ever exhaust the wonder of — and, of course, nothing over which you won't have utterly satisfactory control. And like the lord of the castle who brings out [*ekbállei*] all kinds of things from his treasure [*thēsauroú*] — not only things that were stored up a long time ago but things that were acquired only this morning — you, too, will bring forth things new and old [*kainá kai palaiá*]."

Ekbállei first. The word commonly means "throws out," "casts out," or even "drives out." (Jesus, people said, casts out — *ekbállei* — demons by Beelzebul: Luke 11:15; the Spirit drives — *ekbállei* — Jesus out into the desert: Mark 1:12.) But in addition, it often means "brings out," or "brings forth." ("A good man, out of the good treasure of his heart, brings forth [*ekbállei*] good things," Matt. 12:35.) Therefore, the bringing forth referred to here by Jesus is no rummage-sale unloading of junk; rather, it is a displaying of rare treasures for the fascination of the castle's guests.

And there is a lesson in that for preachers. So often, whether because of thickheadedness, lack of study, scanty preparation, or just plain boredom, they unceremoniously heave the treasures of Scripture out of the pulpit as if they were flopping out so many dead fish. There is no fascination in their monologues, no intrigue, no sense whatsoever that the ministry they have been given is precisely that of being majordomo over a house to end all houses. The most they ever achieve is a kind of monomaniacal enthusiasm for the one or two items that happen to suit their own odd tastes: hellfire, perhaps; or their sawed-off, humanistic version of love; or their short-order recipe for spirituality; or the hopelessly moralistic lessons in good behavior that they long since decided were more palatable than the paradoxes of the

Gospel. There is nothing that resonates with anything like the enthusiasm of, "Hey, look at this fantastic footstool I just discovered!" or, "You've simply got to taste this incredible old Port!" But alas, only that kind of enthusiasm is contagious and joy-producing. We should all pray for them. May God hasten the day on which they will stay in the castle storeroom long enough to get stark staring bonkers about the Word and hilariously drunk on Scripture.

Which brings us to the storeroom itself, the *thēsaurós*, the treasure. We have been shown this treasure once before, hidden in a field. Here, however, it is a treasure finally bought, owned, and manifest. The word *thēsaurós*, incidentally, can denote anything from the stuff you value to the repository you keep it in — and, like the English word "treasure," it can be applied, literally or metaphorically, to almost anything you want. But it is its English derivative "thesaurus," I think, that casts the most light on the way Jesus uses it here.

A thesaurus (as in *Roget's Thesaurus of English Words and Phrases*) is a dictionary of synonyms in which the light of various words and phrases is allowed to shine on practically the whole array of human ideas and concepts. Fascinatingly enough, the entire revelation of God is also just such a thesaurus. The Bible, from start to finish, is a matter of *words;* and even when those words are about *actions* (in particular, when they are about major actions like the Creation, for example, or the choosing of Israel, or the Exodus, or the giving of the Law, or the sacrificial system of the Old Testament — not to mention the Incarnation, or the earthly ministry of Jesus, or his death, resurrection, ascension, or second coming), these actions are presented to us as the work of nothing less than the divine *Word* himself.

It is just that *thēsaurós*, just that treasury of the words of the Word, over which those who have received Jesus' instruction in the mystery of the kingdom have been made *oikodespótai*, lords and masters. And from it, as from an inexhaustible storeroom, they bring forth an endlessly fascinating display of things new and old. How? By the very same method that owners of a literary thesaurus use: by comparing and contrasting what occurs in one place with what the Word says and does in other places. The Bible is not a collection of discrete passages, each of which has only the single meaning it possesses in its isolated spot; rather, it is the vast and unified work of a genius of an author who is constantly cross-referencing himself. Like a first-rate novelist, the Holy Spirit "buries bones" all over the place. Early on, for example, he sneaks in a slain animal that protects the Israelites from the death of the firstborn in Egypt; later, when he is heading for the grand finale, he digs up that bone and turns it, as the Paschal Lamb, into the very crux of his story.

And that is only one illustration out of thousands. There is the tree of life in Eden which surfaces later as both the tree of the cross and the tree for the healing of the nations in the New Jerusalem. There is the virgin conception which, at its first appearance in Isaiah, looks like little more than a political metaphor but which, at the great turning point of the story, reappears as the grand entrance of the Word himself. And there is, to come to one of the most momentous words in Scripture, *blood*, whose imagery grows richer and more complex with each succeeding appearance. From the blood of Abel to the blood on Joseph's coat — to the blood on the doorposts, to the blood of the Old Covenant, to the blood from the Messiah's wounds, to the eucharistic blood of the New Covenant, to the blood of the Lamb in which the saints dip their robes and make them white — there is not a single reference that does not incorporate and enlarge all the meanings that have gone before.

Do you see? The entire revelation is a *thēsaurós* of things new and old that the Spirit is constantly comparing, contrasting, and ringing the changes on. That's why a foolish literalism is such a blind alley. You can't read a great author phrase by phrase as if each word were meant to mean only what it says in the place in which it occurs. Early uses of a word illuminate later ones; and even more important, later uses illuminate earlier ones. Indeed, the Spirit has *all* uses in mind everywhere: he has full and deliberate contol over his story throughout the book. Therefore, unless you wait him out — unless you store up in your own mind a *thēsaurós* of all the bones he has buried — you will make no sense of either the story or its parts. To be sure, many things in the Bible can be taken literally — and just as many can not; but even the literal passages can have nonliteral meanings — and even the nonliteral ones can be utterly crucial to the story.

Therefore, I come back once again to my insistence that, in high seriousness and with equally high glee, we should *play* with Scripture. The *thēsaurós* of the kingdom is not something to be kept in the attic and dragged out only on Sundays for loan exhibitions in museums; nor is it something that people should stare at only when wearing solemn faces and three-piece suits. We may be the *oikodespótai* of the treasure of God, but we were meant first of all to spend huge amounts of time in the attic just poring over it and trying all of it on for size. And we were meant, above all, to invite the world up into the attic to play dress-up with us. We are supposed to be *kids,* you see: "I thank you, Father, Lord of heaven and earth, that you have hidden these things from the wise and prudent, and revealed them to babes." You can't get more encouragement than that for holy horsing around.

And so we come to the end of the passage: what all this playing with the mystery brings forth is *kainá kai palaiá,* things new and old. The treasure of the kingdom does not consist of certain things that are old and certain other things that are new; rather, it consists of old things that are perpetually springing up and new things that turn out to have been around since before the foundation of the world. Pick up any item in it and it will, always and without fail, turn out to be both an antique and a novelty at the same time. And that, when you think of it, is no surprise: the Word who lays up this whole *thēsaurós* for us lays it up first and foremost in the Land of the Trinity where everything is, all at once, older than eternity and as fresh as the breath of the Word who speaks it into being. "Behold, *kainá poiō pánta,* I make all things new," says he who sits, from beginning to end, on the throne of the kingdom. As scribes instructed unto the kingdom of heaven — and as children turned loose in the treasure room of the castle — we've got more than enough to keep us fascinated forever.